Ten Against

Nap

oleon

Douglas Hilt

Nelson-Hall nh Chicago

LIBRARY OF CONGRESS CATALOGING IN PUBLICATION DATA

Hilt, Douglas.
    Ten against Napoleon.

    Bibliography: p.
    Includes index.
    1. Europe—History—1789-1815. 2. Europe—Biog-
raphy. I. Title.
D309.H54   940.2'7'0922   75-9724
ISBN 0-88229-253-6

to
Marquita

Contents

Preface

Few men have dominated their age so completely as did Napoleon. Whatever their conclusions, historians agree that the colossus bestrode his world in all realms—military, political, and social. For a generation following the French Revolution, Napoleon's figure cast a long shadow, from Holland to Egypt, from Moscow to Cádiz. The *Code Napoléon* still remains with us, as do the Arc de Triomphe and the memory of a multi-faceted genius.

Such power and omnipresence exerted an incalculable influence on his European contemporaries. In another more placid era, many of them—writers, artists, politicians, clergymen—would have applied themselves to their calling just as conscientiously but almost certainly less imaginatively. Napoleon's direct intervention into their lives made intellectual escape impossible. Quite unwittingly, his dictatorial methods triggered the release of latent talents and convictions which might otherwise have lain dormant. Thanks to Napoleon's excesses, many of his opponents discovered themselves, rose to new creative heights, became *engagé* in a Sartrean sense.

Some brief examples will suffice. Chateaubriand was shaken out of a narcissistic lethargy, Madame de Staël made Coppet the conscience of Europe, and Schlegel forsook his beloved books to rally to his country's cause. Goya's fullest genius was liberated by Napoleon's invasion, and Pope Pius VII turned crisis into triumph. These are not ineffective, otherworldly romantics, but well-defined individuals in their own right. As such they help correct the erroneous belief that the Romantic was too impractical and escapist to be effective against the apparatus of a modern dictatorship. We have become so dazzled by the central figure of the period that we tend unjustly to overlook the gifted men and women who opposed him. Many of them faced banishment, imprisonment, and grave physical danger, even the possibility of death, details often unknown to the average lay reader.

It would serve little purpose to add to the long list of books dealing with Napoleon himself. Just as the artist or photographer seeks to reveal nuances of character by indirect lighting, so too can the manifold personality of Napoleon be further illuminated by a study of those who came under his influence. In the period from 1799 to 1815, the lives of millions throughout Europe were affected by one man who inspired admiration and enmity, loyalty and distrust—but never indifference. While individual accounts by eyewitnesses are often biased, self-serving, and contradictory, on occasion they reveal a particular insight into Napoleon's character. Such reminiscences have been used in these essays when corroborated by other evidence; to accept the numerous memoirs at face value is to invite self-deception, especially in an age so adept with the pen.

The number of contemporaries could have been extended almost indefinitely, such is the biographical wealth of the period. The selection was necessarily arbitrary and personal; for example, Talleyrand might easily have been substituted for Fouché. Beethoven was omitted only because the story of the *Eroica* symphony is too familiar to bear further retelling. Nor is there any representative from England, not for any lack of personalities—one has only to consider Pitt the Younger, Wellington, and Byron —but because the Channel spared any direct contact with Napoleon and his decrees of exile, censorship, and so forth. It is no accident that the persons chosen were opponents of the self-proclaimed Emperor; their first impression of him, in the majority of cases, had been favorable. The diverse reasons for their growing antipathy disclose not only individual traits but also an intriguing ambivalence in Napoleon's behavior towards his antagonists.

The subjects of the following essays cover a wide range both chronologically and geographically, but in the interest of thematic unity, the scope of the biographies has been largely confined to the Napoleonic period. Pope Pius VII, born in 1740, and Goya, in 1746, are eighteenth-century figures called out of retirement, so to speak, to perform their greatest achievements in a vigorous old age. Chateaubriand, Fouché, Madame de Staël, Constant, Schlegel, Godoy, and Metternich were Napoleon's contemporaries, and the Czar Alexander I, born 1777, was but eight years his junior. Though representing half a dozen nationalities and callings, each was profoundly affected by the decisions of the master of Europe. Most of them outlived the Emperor, and three went on to eminent political careers; yet in each case the Napoleonic years were the most decisive of their lives. By their own admission, what followed was anti-climactic.

Students of the humanities—particularly in the fields of political science, history, and literature—should find this book useful as a supplementary reader that gathers up the complex political, social, and cultural cross-currents of the period. Similarly, the lay reader is offered new insights into the lives and aspirations of a remarkable age. As this work is mainly intended for the non-specialist, I have dispensed with the usual scholarly foot-notes in several languages. For the same reason, all quotations taken from foreign sources have been translated into English. A bibliography to encourage further reading is appended, and a chronological outline is included for easy reference.

I should like to thank Peter Quennell and Alan Hodge, the editors of *History Today,* for their encouragement and permission to reprint material from their publication. In addition, I wish to express my thanks to Mr. Alvaro Cardona-Hine, editor of *Mankind Magazine,* for permission to include the chapter on Fouché. I am also greatly indebted to my wife for having edited and typed the manuscript. Any errors or shortcomings are entirely my own.

Chronology

1740   Future Pope Pius VII born in Cesena in northern Italy.

1746   Francisco Goya born in Fuendetodos, near Saragossa, Aragon, Spain.

1759   Joseph Fouché born in Pellerin, near Nantes.

1766   Germaine de Staël-Holstein born in Paris.

1767   Manuel Godoy born in Badajoz in western Spain. August Wilhelm Schlegel born in Hanover. Benjamin Constant born in Lausanne, Switzerland.

1768   François-René de Chateaubriand born in St. Malo, Brittany.

1769   Napoleon Bonaparte born in Ajaccio, Corsica, ceded to France by the Republic of Genoa the previous year.

1773   Clemens Metternich born in Coblenz on the Rhine.

1777   Future Czar Alexander I born in St. Petersburg.

1788   Charles IV and María Luisa ascend the Spanish throne.

1789   Outbreak of the French Revolution.

1792   Francis II of Austria becomes Holy Roman Emperor.

1793   Execution of Louis XVI and Marie Antoinette. Napoleon assists in defense of Toulon.

Chronology

1795	Napoleon saves the Convention during the coup of Vendémiaire.
1796-	Napoleon marries Josephine Beauharnais.
1797	First Italian campaign. Paul I Czar of Russia ascends throne.
1798-	Egyptian campaign. Napoleon returns to France,
1799	becomes First Consul through coup d'état of Brumaire.
1800	Pius VII elected Pope.
1801	Concordat signed. Alexander I becomes Czar upon assassination of Paul I.
1804	Execution of duc d'Enghien. Napoleon crowned Emperor.
1805	Battles of Trafalgar (October) and Austerlitz (December).
1806	Dissolution of the Holy Roman Empire.
1808	Invasion of Spain. Abdication of Charles IV and María Luisa, fall of Godoy.
1809	Abduction of Pope Pius VII by the French.
1810	Napoleon marries Marie Louise following divorce from Josephine.
1812	Disaster of Grande Armée in Russia.
1813	Defeat of Napoleon at Leipzig (Battle of the Nations).
1814	Pope Pius VII released from captivity. First abdication of Napoleon, exile to Elba.
1815	Hundred Days end at Waterloo, banishment to St. Helena.
1817	Death of Madame de Staël in Paris.

1820   Death of Fouché in Trieste.

1821   Death of Napoleon on St. Helena.

1823   Death of Pope Pius VII in Rome.

1825   Death of Czar Alexander I in Taganrog, Crimea.

1828   Death of Francisco Goya in Bordeaux.

1830   Death of Benjamin Constant in Paris.

1845   Death of August Wilhelm Schlegel in Bonn.

1848   Death of Chateaubriand in Paris.

1851   Death of Manuel Godoy in Paris.

1852   Napoleon's nephew declared Emperor Napoleon III.

1859   Death of Metternich in Vienna.

Introduction

In Molière's *Le Tartuffe,* the wily protagonist does not appear in person until the play is nearly half over. Yet even off-stage, his unseen presence dominates everything—the lives, the thoughts, and the actions of those who come into contact with him. In much the same way, from his accession to power through the coup d'état of 18 Brumaire (November 9, 1799) to his final banishment to St. Helena, Napoleon commanded the attention of a continent. Though often absent from his capital, he remained the cynosure of all Europe wherever he conducted his campaigns. Decisions of state—both major and inconsequential—were made from afar; from East Prussia he once roundly scolded his Minister of Police for failing to evict Mme de Staël from Paris. We are dealing with a dictator and, as the following essays make clear, not a particularly benevolent one. But Napoleon was far more than another brash usurper, for he was also the successor of the Enlightenment and the French Revolution.

In part, Napoleon's uncertain attitude towards this dual inheritance explains his ambivalent conduct towards his opponents. Should he appear generous or harsh, benevolent or unforgiving? Imperious by nature, he was forced in the early years of the Consulate to dissimulate and—at least outwardly—observe democratic procedures. As early as 1799, Napoleon recognized a salient fact which had escaped the attention of the military and ex-Jacobins: the Revolution was over, and the people wanted order, not liberty. The average citizen was tired of corruption, inflation, and food shortages; revolutionary rhetoric was no substitute for bread. A growing nostalgia for the old days was increasingly evident, an attachment to the old festivals and saints' days and a wish to rest once a week instead of observing the ten-day *décadi* of the new calendar. When Bonaparte (to give him his correct name at this point) declared, "Citizens, the revolution is tied to the principles that gave it birth: it is over with," all understood the sense, if not the syntax. The new constitution—France's fourth in ten years—was endorsed by a huge majority of the nation; Bonaparte did not even wait for the votes to be counted before naming the two new Consuls, and through them, the Senate and other legislators. The first nominations, such as the appointment of Benjamin Constant to the Tribunate, were generally liberal, but the façade gave little more than a republican appearance to a dictatorial reality.

Needless to say, all real power was concentrated in the person of the First Consul. No opposition was brooked, but a sincere attempt was made to incorporate men of ability, no matter what their past actions. With his customary cynicism, on this occasion Bonaparte could claim with justice: "What revolutionary won't have confidence in a system where Fouché will be a minister? What gentleman won't wish to live under the former Bishop of Autun [Talleyrand]? The one protects my left, the other my right. I am opening up a highway where all may reach the end." These two devious talents were typical of similar ministerial appointments; pragmatism took precedence over rigid philosophy.

Though Bonaparte had been granted extraordinary powers that gave him control over domestic and foreign policy (including taxation and new legislation), the period up to the end of 1802 was generally one of moderation. True, there had been a spectacular assassination attempt against him on Christmas Eve, 1800, when a *machine infernale* exploded as he was on his way to the opera; the First Consul seized the chance to deport fifty of his potential enemies, despite their innocence. Many of his generals, hitherto companions in arms, resented his rapid rise and sought to overthrow the Corsican upstart. All attempts to unseat him were foiled, but it was only the constitutional amendment of August 1802—another plebiscite ensuring a huge majority—which proclaimed him First Consul for life that gave him full assurance. The elevation to Emperor was but a later refinement.

Having restored confidence to a country rent with disorder and on the verge of bankruptcy, Bonaparte was able to deal with the scattered royalist forces (mainly in the west) and to recoup the lost territories in Italy. Only the envious or the adherents of an effective constitution raised their voices in hesitant protest, and even these were briefly stilled after the victory at Marengo. At first, a defeat had been reported, but confirmation of the good news was greeted with spontaneous enthusiasm, the public believing that after a decade of sacrifice the revolutionary wars were now at an end. The treaties of Lunéville and Amiens—the latter bringing peace with England —seemed to confirm this; France had achieved her natural frontiers, and a long era of tranquility was at hand. Bonaparte's popularity had reached its zenith.

Parisian society had long recovered from the trauma of the Reign of Terror and had acquired some bizarre forms, notably the outrageously dressed *incroyables* and an impressive number of gambling and dance halls. On a more staid level, the salons made a cautious reappearance, providing Mme de Staël and her confidante, Mme Récamier, with congenial centers from which to disseminate their liberal ideas. The homes of Mme Talma, the close friend of Benjamin Constant and wife of a famous actor, and Mme Tallien were frequented by a vast concourse of admirers. Bonaparte generally regarded such social magnets with disdain and suspicion, but his brothers Joseph and Lucien, with cheerful nonchalance, were among the most frequent habitués.

As a group, women gained very little from the Napoleonic era. The First Consul regarded woman as the property of man much as "a gooseberry bush is the property of the gardener," and the *Code Napoléon* specifically decreed that a wife must obey her husband. In an age of extremely relaxed morals, such optimistic expectations were impossible to enforce. The result can be imagined; with Napoleon's headstrong sisters setting the pace, society ladies went their own way. Generally speaking, Napoleon's commands were better obeyed on the battlefield than in the boudoir.

The first visible divergence from the spirit of the revolution was the conclusion of the Concordat with Pope Pius VII. The Church, as a link to the past, was back in favor, but it would be a mistake to attribute this to any deep religious fervor. It was more a sentimental religiosity, a lyrical mysticism à la Chateaubriand. On Easter

Day 1802, the bells of Notre Dame rang out after ten years' silence, and the three Consuls dutifully attended Mass. The Concordat was essentially an astute but cynical act to unify the people for political purposes, in Robiquet's phrase, "to reassure their consciences so as better to enslave them, that was the idea behind the maneuver." On the one hand, Bonaparte weaned away many of the parish priests from the royalists; on the other, he strengthened his own power vis-à-vis the Church. His coronation in December 1804, during which he humiliated the Pope by seizing the imperial crown and placing it on his own head, symbolized the new reality; the state reasserted its supremacy over the Church, while the onlookers were left in no doubt as to who ruled the state. Although Napoleon's uncle was already a cardinal, Pope Pius VII was arrested in 1809 for political reasons and imprisoned in France for five years. The Emperor was excommunicated, but by then was beyond such trifling matters.

Bonaparte's early measures were impressive, both political and domestic. Communications between cities were improved, and a start was made to bring the brigands who had terrorized the countryside under control (even so, the carriage of one of Napoleon's mistresses was held up at pistol point). Travel was still slow and uncertain, but in 1804, the *vélocifères* were introduced, placing Rouen within seven hours of Paris. Despite the sufferings and uncertainties that lay before them, most people with means were inveterate travelers; Chateaubriand made the journey to Venice as a septuagenarian, while Goya crossed the Pyrenees at the age of eighty-two. The accommodations were often rough and the cuisine deplorable, but compared to the transcontinental marches that Napoleon's foot-soldiers were forced to endure, such travel was relatively luxurious. Journeys were by horse, carriage, or sailing ship; timetables were more optimistic than accurate, and the whole experience marked by a cheerful camaraderie. The mail service was expensive and erratic, due in part to the unpredictable censorship.

Paris, like most cities at the beginning of the nineteenth century, was still unhygienic and malodorous. The Seine was little more than an open sewer, a fertile breeding ground for the diseases that periodically swept the city. Flooding was common, but there was often a shortage of drinking water, and few people took regular baths. Napoleon instituted several improvements, but it was left to his nephew in mid-century to alter the face of the city. The imperial style changed the tone of society and introduced a declamatory vogue in furniture and decorations; little attention was paid to the more basic comforts. The bathrooms remained primitive, and constant drafts and the fragrance of indoor flowers were relied upon to dispel unpleasant odors. Heating was rudimentary, lighting mostly by candle. Though the proclamation of the Empire implied a certain elegance of manners and protocol, the everyday reality showed little change; even Napoleon frequently attended morning receptions in his night clothes until the rooms had warmed up a little. The domestic conveniences flowing from the Industrial Revolution still lay ahead, and comfort had to be derived from gargantuan meals that lasted for hours and the scintillating conversation that was an essential part of them.

From its inception, the new régime instituted censorship of the press and theatre. Far from being a precision instrument, it was arbitrary and inefficient, despite occasional ruthlessness. As Minister of Police, Fouché used discretion and moderation, preferring prevention to cruelty. Mme de Staël remarked that he chose the good "because it was reasonable, and his intelligence at times led him to the same results that others would have

reached under the inspiration of their conscience." Nevertheless, the cold-blooded execution of Chateaubriand's
cousin showed the darker side of Fouché's enigmatic
character. His successor, General Savary, made no pretense of being humane; "If I ordered Savary to get rid
of his wife and children," Napoleon reportedly said, "I
am sure he would not hesitate." Repressive measures
taken against enemies of the régime varied greatly, ranging from expulsion from the Tribunate—as in the case of
Benjamin Constant—to exile, imprisonment, or the death
sentence. When war was resumed with England on May
18, 1803, Napoleon interned some 7,000 hapless English
tourists who found themselves stranded in France. Today, we have become inured to such practices and to far
worse, but such treatment at the time was regarded as
barbaric.

The newspapers reflected the policy of the government, and Chateaubriand's critical article in the *Mercure*
was not allowed to become a daily occurrence. Literary
standards declined, and a pretentious rhetorical style became all-pervasive, originating, no doubt, in the over-
blown language of the victory bulletins. Of the writers
during the Napoleonic period, only Chateaubriand, Mme
de Staël, and Constant are memorable, and it is significant
that all three were critics of the régime. The theatre,
though very popular and boasting actors of the talent of
Talma and Mlle George—a personal favorite of the Emperor—has bequeathed nothing of note. Some of the live-
lier scenes took place in the parterre between rival
claques and cliques, each one considering itself the ultimate authority in the correct interpretation of a classic
role, and not sparing in vocal advice. Certain plays were
banned altogether on unspecified grounds, while some of
Corneille's verses were improved upon so as to depict
the Empire in the best possible light. The censorship was

more erratic than severe, as much moral as political, and imposed at least in part by the public. No cuckolds, divorces, or seductions were allowed to be depicted; one cynic observed that "one must have virtue on the stage, because there must be some somewhere." No worthwhile original plays were produced; if literature reflects its period, there can be no more accurate indictment of the era.

The first three years of Napoleon's rule, though disquieting to constitutionalists grounded in the English tradition, were characterized by general progress. Food was plentiful again, and prices stabilized. The new civil code produced a uniform legal system that made the family once more the center of society. The war with England was remote, and military service could be avoided by a bribe or desertion. Conscription was of recent origin, but even so, Napoleon's first armies were small compared to those of the later campaigns. Yet not all was well, and the first cracks soon appeared in the imposing façade.

It had long become clear that Bonaparte had no intention of inviting the Bourbons back. Notwithstanding the Concordat, the royalist plots to regain the throne multiplied, but Fouché's spies had little trouble scotching them. An ambitious attempt by Cadoudal and General Pichegru, both supplied with English funds, was more serious as a national hero, General Moreau, apparently was involved. The trap was sprung and the three men arrested; Cadoudal was executed, Pichegru died mysteriously in his cell, and Moreau—though innocent—was sent into exile. Napoleon still was not content, and ordered the arrest of the duc d'Enghien, a Bourbon prince of the Condé family, whom he mistakenly held responsible for the plot. The Duke was residing in Ettenheim across the Rhine on German territory, but he nevertheless was seized and brought to the fortress of Vincennes near Paris. Following a mockery of a court-martial presided over by Napoleon's brother-in-law—the sentence had already been decided before any evidence was presented—the uncomprehending young man was led to the moat and executed by a waiting firing squad. The castle ditch was Napoleon's Rubicon; the news of this deliberate murder united Europe against the tyrant.

The splendor of the Pope's extended visit and the coronation in Notre Dame belied the hastening tragedy brought on by the Emperor's hubris. The glittering veneer of the Empire, the systematic plundering of Europe's art treasures to fill the Louvre—renamed the Musée Napoléon—and a succession of brilliant land victories made France the undisputed center of power on the Continent. Austria and Prussia had been decisively defeated at Ulm and Jena, while Russia suffered major disasters at Austerlitz and Friedland. To Napoleon's chagrin, these triumphs were received with little real enthusiasm by the majority of Frenchmen. Memories were still fresh of a recent financial crisis occasioned in part by growing war expenditures, and the demands for new conscripts became increasingly onerous. As the conflict spread to Spain and Portugal in 1808, France acquired the appearance of a vast barracks. The slaughter at the Pyrrhic victory of Eylau, and the surrender of a whole army at Bailén in Andalucia presaged the end to any assumed invincibility on the battlefield; nor could the dramatic meeting with Czar Alexander on a raft near Tilsit conceal a growing discord. War had become a way of life.

The area of hostilities now stretched from the Atlantic to the Baltic, and Napoleon was forced to delegate command to other generals, some gifted but many venal and incompetent. Often the imperial armies resembled some swollen foreign legion drawn from the conquered territories; the Grand Army that advanced into Russia in

1812 was less than half French. The precarious foundations of the imperial edifice became evident during Napoleon's absence in Moscow. A General Malet, recently released from an insane asylum, spread the rumor that the Emperor was dead. Savary was arrested, and the flimsy conspiracy might well have succeeded but for a stroke of bad luck. Napoleon hurried back to Paris, leaving the remains of his army to its fate on the Russian steppes.

Despite lowering the age limit for military service and scouring the countryside for deserters, the need for soldiers was insatiable. A vicious guerrilla war in Spain required thousands of garrison troops, while the outbreak of a national uprising in Germany following the disastrous retreat from Russia consumed one army after another. The size of the forces thrown into battle also escalated; the engagement at Leipzig—known in Germany as the Battle of the Nations—was enormous in scope and duration, involving over half a million men and lasting from October 16-19, 1813.

The situation within France became desperate. Though well administered by the efficient prefect system, Napoleon's exactions placed an intolerable load on the country. The failure of the Continental System, a blockade designed to bring England to her knees by denying the sale of her products abroad, resulted in an active contraband and higher prices for overseas goods; the poor wheat harvests of 1811 and 1812 caused widespread speculation as grain was withheld from the open market. Clashes between soldiers and civilians became more frequent; the nation was exhausted, and no longer believed in Napoleon's star. The Emperor's abdication on April 4, 1814 was greeted with general relief, and the restoration of the Bourbons with resigned indifference.

On the heels of the allied armies there followed two other contingents comprised of the émigrés who had not returned previously and the opponents whom Napoleon had exiled. A deep conflict between the two groups soon became apparent; in Talleyrand's immortal phrase, the Bourbons had "learned nothing and forgotten nothing," whereas the political exiles tended to be progressive in outlook. Louis XVIII personally was content to forgive and forget, being perfectly willing to bestow a constitutional charter to the nation he had not seen for a quarter century. His immediate entourage, however, deeply resented this imagined restriction to the royal power, and was further infuriated by the retention of a host of Napoleonic administrators and ministers, including Talleyrand and Fouché. It was not long before a large segment of Frenchmen became disillusioned by the vindictiveness and pettiness of the Bourbons, and soon longing glances were cast in the direction of the island of Elba to which Napoleon had been banished.

The ex-Emperor was kept well informed of developments on the mainland. He had been permitted to retain a minuscule army and a reduced court, generously subsidized by the victors. The Empress Marie Louise, who had succeeded Josephine in 1810, refused to join her husband, but Napoleon was adequately consoled by a visit from Marie Walewska, his Polish mistress. The Allies had meanwhile established themselves in Vienna where, amid lavish balls and pleasurable pursuits, they drew up the future of Europe. The dominant figures at the Congress were Czar Alexander and Metternich, the Austrian Minister of Foreign Affairs who had negotiated the marriage between Napoleon and Marie Louise. They were later joined by Talleyrand, who quickly imposed his diplomatic talents on the other participants. Suddenly the banquets and deliberations were interrupted by the news of Napoleon's landing on the French mainland. The Bourbon army melted away, and soon the "Corsican ogre" was installed once more at the Tuileries.

The hurried events of the Hundred Days bewildered most of the participants. Uncertain of the future, the majority were either opportunists or fatalists. Fouché and Constant remained to serve the Emperor, each in his peculiar way, while Chateaubriand and Talleyrand staked their futures on the Bourbons. The average citizen prayed that he could keep pace with the latest change in fortune; in Robiquet's words, "if it is true that a fool is one who never changes his mind, then France has never had so many intelligent citizens as between 1814 and 1815." Napoleon's decisive defeat at Waterloo and permanent exile to distant St. Helena settled matters conclusively. Though almost immediately there began the weaving of the imperial myth at which the ex-Emperor was so adept, nothing following the second Bourbon restoration could prevent the royalist vengeance known as the White Terror from sweeping the country. Such was its fury that not even Fouché survived in office for long.

Properly speaking, our chronicle should close with the year 1815. Those who had opposed Napoleon openly were now beyond his reach. Pope Pius VII had been freed from captivity in March 1814, and the other exiles were now at liberty to resume their interrupted careers. In Spain, with the return of Fernando VII, the Desired, a new terror established itself as the vengeful king sought to eradicate the liberals. Chateaubriand, as Foreign Minister in 1823, unwittingly exacerbated the tragedy by dispatching a French army to intervene on behalf of the temporarily beleaguered king. With the exception of such minor revolts, Europe was about to enter a long period of peace, conducive, among other things, to the writing of exculpating memoirs. Often the wheel turned full circle; many of those who had first admired Bonaparte, only to endure privations at his hands, came to regard him in later years with a certain admiration, even nostalgia. They had suffered much, yet they knew that theirs had been a most uncommon foe. To have lived in an aura of greatness, there is much one forgives.

François-René de
Chateaubriand

"I arrived in this world twenty days after Bonaparte; he brought me with him." Factually, Chateaubriand's statement is incorrect; he was born in 1768 and the future Emperor a year later, but there was literary, if not literal, truth in his assertion. An enemy of despotism but a venerator of grandeur, Chateaubriand was unable— indeed, unwilling—to break away from the figure whose all-encompassing power at once repelled and attracted him. In his autobiographical *Mémoires d'Outre-Tombe*, a vainglorious literary monument to himself, Chateaubriand wistfully recalls: "Descending from Bonaparte and the Empire to those who followed them, is like falling from reality into the void, from the summit of a mountain into an abyss." Thus the homage of the greatest French writer of the age to its dominating personality.

Though politically opposed to one another from 1804 until the Emperor's ultimate downfall, there is a curious identification, even admiration, that runs parallel through their careers. It is with honest pride that Napoleon's encomium, dictated on St. Helena, is reproduced in the *Mémoires*: "Chateaubriand has received the sacred fire from Nature; his works bear witness to it. His style is not that of Racine but that of the prophet." The recipient of this welcome flattery hastens to add: "Why shouldn't I admit that this opinion 'tickles my heart's proud weakness'? Many little men to whom I have rendered great services have not judged me as favorably as the giant whose might I had dared attack." These are the generous sentiments expressed after a decade of opposition; to place them in truer perspective one must return to the beginning of the century.

The first months of 1800 found Napoleon's position as First Consul far from secure. It was his great—if fortunate—victory at Marengo on June 14 that scattered the enemy as effectively at home as abroad. Thus began a remarkable era of victory bulletins, overwhelming plebescites of support, climaxed in 1804 by a magnificent Coronation at which Pope Pius VII officiated. Faced with such power and splendor, how dare a mere writer measure himself against the imperial might? Yet this was to be Chateaubriand's chosen destiny.

No doubt the first thirty years of Chateaubriand's life were more romantic in the later emotional recollection than in the actual living. Following an unhappy and sickly childhood in Brittany, François-René had been presented to the Court at Versailles as the son of a minor aristocratic family. A chance witness to the fall of the Bastille, he had been quick to comprehend the historic implications. His dreamy and romantic disposition released a wanderlust that took him to the virgin forests of

America, where supposedly he familiarized himself with Indian customs. At the news of Louis XVI's arrest, the young Breton monarchist hastened back to France, a poorly-timed decision made worse by an ill-considered marriage. He soon bade a not reluctant farewell to his bride and joined the émigré army, to be wounded almost immediately at the siege of Thionville. There followed seven years of exile in England, separated from wife and family, a period of poverty and frustration while teaching French and writing inconsequential essays.

The tragic news of the execution of the King was soon followed by that of Chateaubriand's elder brother and the arrest of his mother. An impossible love for a clergyman's daughter added emotional suffering to the daily pangs of hunger and loss of identity in an alien world. Though still a monarchist, his childhood religious faith had been shattered, and nothing had taken its place. At this time of inner crisis, he met Louis de Fontanes, a fellow exile, who not only restored his personal faith—a task made more acute by the news of the deaths of Chateaubriand's mother and his sister Julie—but who also convinced him that France was eager to reject the atheism and rationalist deism of the Revolution. It was from such encouragement that *Le Génie du Christianisme* (*The Spirit of Christianity*), an inspired amalgam of religion amid sympathetic nature, came into being. With this manuscript in his trunk, Chateaubriand crossed the Channel in May 1800: "We took four hours to cross over from Dover to Calais. I slipped into my country protected by a foreign name: doubly hidden in the obscurity of the Swiss Lassagne and my own, I entered France with the century."

Like most monarchists, he viewed Bonaparte's ascendancy with enthusiasm, regarding him as the restorer of order from chaos, and hopefully as the French Monck

3

who would invite the exiled Bourbons to regain their throne. On arrival in Paris, his first problem was to have his name removed from the list of émigrés, and his obvious intermediary was his former friend in London, Louis de Fontanes. Not only was he closely acquainted with Napoleon's brother, Lucien, but he had also secured their sister Elisa as his mistress. Fontanes had recently been appointed editor of the *Mercure de France* and invited Chateaubriand to contribute a brief article which contained an ill-judged outburst directed against Mme de Staël. Characteristically, the latter bore the author no grudge and was soon addressing him (in English) as "my dear Francis." No harm was done, and Chateaubriand even acquired a modest fame from the incident.

Despite Fontanes' enthusiasm, the religious climate in France was not quite as favorable as the two friends had hoped. The ex-revolutionaries such as Fouché—now Minister of Police—and the majority of Bonaparte's comrades in arms were resolutely opposed to any such restoration. The First Consul wavered between cynicism and political opportunism, having flattered the Muslims in Egypt one year and then celebrated a *Te Deum* after Marengo the next. He was shrewd enough to realize that religion afforded a moral and disciplinary foundation to the state; why then antagonize a potential ally? To one group of royalists he admitted candidly: "I intend to reestablish religion, not for your sakes but for mine." Chateaubriand astutely decided to publish the *Atala* episode taken from the much longer *Génie du Christianisme*; the result was a brilliant success that perfectly answered the nation's spiritual needs. The new century had acquired its first masterpiece: lyricism, religion, and an exotic setting had been marvelously fused in the brief story of the Indian maiden's pathetic sacrifice. If Chateaubriand helped religion regain its former popularity, then certainly it was religion in turn that made him famous. Henceforward—and often to his great embarrassment—Chateaubriand was regarded as France's most representative Catholic author.

The fact was that this eloquent Defender of the Faith had made no attempt to encourage his wife to join him in Paris—far from it, he was now enjoying life with his mistress, Pauline, Mme de Beaumont. Together they worked on the preparation of the full *Génie du Christianisme,* which included a section extolling the sanctity of marriage. The work is a poetic paean that "proves" the superiority of the Christian faith largely through an artistic appeal to the senses; sculpture, literature, Gothic cathedrals, even agriculture, are presented as evidence of God's purpose. The beauty of the Church's ritual, the emotions released by the sound of the bells—all testify to an essential truth. Lucien Bonaparte added some vacuous notes in the margin of the manuscript, but Mme de Staël, alighting on the chapter headed *"De la Virginité,"* called on her vast experience to exclaim: "My goodness! Our poor Chateaubriand! That's going to fall flat on its face!" Napoleon, less concerned with such details, considered the publication of the work fortuitous; the Concordat was promulgated on April 8, 1802, and the *Génie du Christianisme* was published six days later. To show his gratitude, Chateaubriand dedicated the second edition to the First Consul, "the brilliant Bonaparte whom Providence has marked from afar for the accomplishment of his prodigious plans"—a panegyric that the author's enemies would often recall in the future.

No matter how shallow its theology, the popularity of the book served the purpose of both writer and First Consul, as Chateaubriand frankly acknowledged:

> Bonaparte, wishing at that time to base his power on the foundation of society, had just come to an agreement with the Court of Rome; at first he placed no obstacle in the way of the publication of a work useful to the popularity of his plans; he had to struggle against the men surrounding him and against the declared enemies of religion; he was therefore glad to be defended from without by public opinion derived from the *Génie du Christianisme.*

Not surprisingly, Chateaubriand's name was removed from the proscribed list of émigrés; surely a dazzling literary and political career lay before him. Soon after the proclamation of the Concordat, Lucien invited his friend to a reception at which he met Napoleon for the first time. The first impression was positive, even lyrical: "His smile was caressing and beautiful, his glance admirable, especially the way in which his eyes were placed beneath his forehead and framed by his eyebrows. As yet there was no charlatanism in his look, nothing theatrical or affected." To Chateaubriand, the explanation was self-evident: "The *Génie du Christianisme,* which at that moment was causing a great stir, had acted upon Napoleon." An affable discussion followed, ranging from Egypt to Christianity and astronomy. It was the last pleasant exchange between the two men.

The anticipated diplomatic appointment took longer than expected. Chateaubriand decided to face the inevitable and reconcile himself with his wife after a separation of ten years; public Christians must be prepared to make visible sacrifices. Finally, on May 4, 1803, he was appointed Secretary to the French delegation in Rome; the new Ambassador to the Holy See was to be Cardinal Fesch, Napoleon's uncle. Chateaubriand was urged to accept the subordinate post by the Abbé Emery *"pour le bien de la religion."* In a more candid moment, he assured the aspiring diplomat that he would soon be in charge, as

Fesch was none too intelligent—an unfortunate assumption, as events proved.

The first few weeks in Rome exceeded all expectations. An audience with Pope Pius VII, "pale, sad and religious, the real Pontiff of Tribulations," was a great success; a copy of the *Génie* was considerately open on the Pope's table and formed the basis of their discussion. Regrettably, this early good fortune went to Chateaubriand's head, and he deemed it his duty to visit the ex-King of Sardinia, a declared enemy of the French Republic. Cardinal Fesch was furious and reported this grave diplomatic error to his nephew, but as the offender readily admitted, "fortunately, I was dealing with Bonaparte; what should have drowned me, saved me." A visit from the First Consul's sister, the sensuous Pauline Borghese, on the slender pretext of accepting a pair of shoes, was not unwelcome: "I was introduced to her; she did her toilette in front of me," we are told in the *Mémoires*. Such pleasurable moments did little to alleviate the boredom and growing friction between the impetuous Secretary and the insufferable prelate. The lingering illness and death of Mme de Beaumont, whom he cared for during her last sufferings in Rome, decided matters for him. He had heard of a diplomatic opening in the Canton de Valais which, though modest, would secure his freedom.

Though Fontanes had become President of the Legislative Body, Chateaubriand readily admitted that he owed this unexpected opportunity to Napoleon's intervention:

> While I wavered between a thousand resolutions, I received the news that the First Consul had appointed me Minister to the Valais. He had first flown into a rage on the basis of some denunciations; but returning to his senses, he understood that I belonged to that race that that can only act in the first rank, that I should not be

7

mixed with others, or otherwise I could never be used to advantage. There was no place vacant; he created one, and choosing it in conformity with my instinct for solitude and independence, he placed me in the Alps; he gave me a Catholic republic amid a world of torrents. . . .

Very prettily expressed; but Chateaubriand realized that such poetic sentiments did not correspond to the reality of the situation. Once again France was at war with England, and Fouché was kept busy unearthing royalist conspiracies.

On March 19, 1804, the newly-appointed Chargé d'affaires went to the Tuileries to take leave of the First Consul before taking up his post; a dismaying change had taken place since their last meeting two years previously:

As he approached me, I was struck by the alteration in his face: his cheeks were sunken and livid, his eyes hard, his complexion pale and blotchy, his look gloomy and terrible. The attraction, which had previously impelled me towards him, ceased; instead of remaining in his line of advance, I made a movement to avoid him. He threw a glance at me as if he were trying to recognize me, took a few steps toward me, then turned round and walked away. Had I appeared to him as a warning?

Already one can perceive the peculiar fusion of Chateaubriand with the historic figure he affects to reject, the use of literature to create the illusion of reality, the studied pose for posterity. The further apart the two men drifted politically, the closer they came spiritually.

Two days later, Napoleon's confused behavior became clear to all; the newspapers announced the summary arrest, trial and execution of the duc d'Enghien, a Bourbon prince. The evidence of the Duke's involvement in any conspiracy was nonexistent, his arrest in Germany a breach of international law, and his trial a legal travesty. His death caused widespread revulsion throughout

Europe, but in a cruel sense also cleared the air, marking the final break between Bonaparte and the Bourbons. To Chateaubriand, the Duke's judicial murder gave a well-defined cause that he had previously lacked; henceforth he would loudly proclaim the legitimist principle, whatever ridicule or personal disadvantage it might incur. Without a moment's hesitancy, he penned his letter of resignation, addressing it to Talleyrand, the Minister of Foreign Relations, who fortunately had the good sense to withhold it from his master for several days. Even though Chateaubriand pleaded his wife's alleged poor health as his principal reason, nevertheless his action required considerable courage and self-sacrifice. It marked the decisive turning point in the careers of both men; the Bonaparte whom Chateaubriand had often admired became the Napoleon whose power he would oppose. Hitherto servile, he was now a free man:

> The death of the duc d'Enghien had for me the advantage that, by thrusting me aside, it left me to follow my own inspiration in solitude and prevented me from enlisting in the regular infantry of old Pindus: I owed my intellectual liberty to my moral liberty.

Six weeks after, Napoleon declared himself Emperor. Perhaps feeling that the occasion called for magnanimity rather than retribution, he even teased his sister Elisa: "You were quite worried about your friend!" Fontanes and Chateaubriand's other acquaintances remained loyal to him, and no restrictions were placed on his movements. Indeed, Chateaubriand's criticism was now directed at the same Pope who had so courteously received him at the Vatican, for agreeing to perform the coronation, thereby sanctifying Napoleon and the Empire. Secretly, the elevation of his adversary also raised Chateaubriand in his own self-esteem:

But in daring to leave Bonaparte, I had placed myself at his level.... Until his fall, he held the sword suspended over my head; sometimes he would return to me due to a natural inclination and he would try to drown me in his fatal success; sometimes I was inclined towards him by the admiration he inspired in me, by the idea that I was witnessing a transformation of society and not simply a change of dynasty: but so hostile in many respects, our two natures would then reassert themselves again, and if he would gladly have had me shot, I would not have felt much sorrow in killing him either.

No shooting took place, and the romantic author-hero was reduced to the prosaic task of earning a living by his pen.

Finding his head still on his shoulders, Chateaubriand began research in preparation for his *Martyrs de Dioclétien*; if Napoleon refused to make him a martyr, well then, he would have to write about others. The work was a natural outgrowth from the *Génie*; the theme of barren paganism contrasted with the inspirational wonders of Christianity struck the author as one of great immediacy. Moreover, the work entailed would assuage the sorrow he felt on the suicide of his sister Lucile following a tragic life, and his dismay at the ostentation that marked the Coronation in December. The first draft was soon completed, but Chateaubriand felt that it failed to reveal his unique cachet, the poetic coloration that could only result from personal immersion in the exotic world described, the technique which had made *Atala* such a success. A generous gift from the Empress, the wife of Czar Alexander I of Russia—romantic mystics themselves—made the projected visit to the Holy Land possible, and in June 1806 he set out with his wife. Alas! her health failed her in Venice and she was forced to turn back. Fortunately, Chateaubriand had foreseen such a mishap and had made advance preparations; Natalie de Noailles, his current mistress, had been instructed to meet the pilgrim in Spain to help relieve the rigors of the tour. Once again, the alluring landscapes in Greece and Palestine released the impressionist word painter, who took the opportunity to follow Bonaparte's earlier path along the littoral as far as Alexandria before turning south to gaze at the Pyramids. Having survived a storm of romantic intensity, Chateaubriand arrived in Spain towards the end of March 1807, a year before Napoleon's invasion of the Peninsula. His meeting with Natalie is gallantly omitted from the *Mémoires;* the journey home was unhurried.

Following his return to France, he acquired ownership of the prestigious *Mercure,* probably with secret royalist funds. The moment for an effective thrust at the absent Emperor seemed especially propitious; the battle of Eylau in East Prussia against the Russians (February 8, 1807), though unhesitatingly claimed by Napoleon as yet another victory, had resulted in tremendous losses on both sides, and word of the carnage had filtered back to Paris. On July 4, 1807, appeared a defiant article under Chateaubriand's name in the *Mercure,* denouncing the evils of despotism:

> When amid the silence of abjection only the echo of the slave's chains and the informer's voice is heard; when all tremble before the tyrant, and where it is as dangerous to incur his favor as to deserve his displeasure, the historian appears, entrusted with the vengeance of the nations. Nero prospers in vain, Tacitus is already born within the Empire; he grows up, unrecognized, beside the ashes of Germanicus, and already a just Providence has entrusted the glory of the world's master to a child. If the historian's role is lofty, it is also dangerous....

"If Napoleon was through with the kings, he was not through with me," Chateaubriand noted while awaiting the imperial thunderbolt. Nor was it an humbled Napoleon who returned to Paris; the victory at Friedland and the subsequent conference with the Czar at Tilsit had enabled him to recoup his prestige. Upon his arrival, Cardinal Fesch showed his nephew the offending article which, to make matters worse, had received Mme de Staël's approval. Napoleon's wrath was of true imperial proportions, including a threat to have his sniping critic cut down with sabers on the steps of the Tuileries. Less colorful, but more practical, was the imposition of a sterner censorship.

Some months later, Napoleon took the opportunity to view his opponent's portrait by Girodet on display at the Salon. The likeness—curiously Napoleonic in its awkward pose—faithfully reproduced Chateaubriand's Mediterranean suntan, which elicited the remark that "he looks like a conspirator coming down the chimney." Other than an unofficial banishment to the countryside, Napoleon maliciously understood that a daily tongue-lashing from Mme Chateaubriand—a great admirer of the Emperor—was punishment enough.

After years of preparation, the *Martyrs de Dioclétien* was finally published in March 1809. Aside from the evocative landscapes and lyrical passages, the work to a certain extent is a *roman à clef*. The proconsul Hiéroclès, an ex-Christian turned cruel atheist, is recognizable as Fouché. In all fairness, the Minister of Police had generously suggested that the author censor his own treatise, which largely explains his anger on discovering the unflattering literary portrait. Chateaubriand's timing could not have been worse. Recently, his cousin Armand had been captured with incriminating papers while attempting a secret landing on the Normandy coast. Immediately brought to Paris as a royalist spy, his arrest was the answer to Fouché's prayers (if such an expression can be applied to a nonbeliever). Chateaubriand lamented:

> Armand had the wind, the waves and the imperial police against him; Bonaparte was in league with the storms. The gods spent a great amount of anger against such a paltry existence.

Despite the intercession of the Empress Josephine, Napoleon stubbornly supported Fouché in this matter, even though he had fallen out with his minister on most others. "What did it concern Napoleon to have insects crushed by his own hand on his crown?" To underline his contempt, Armand was executed by a firing squad on Good Friday.

Events and personal fortunes changed rapidly under the Empire. By the following year, Fouché had been replaced as Minister of Police by Savary, and the barren Josephine by Marie Louise. The new royal union required a certain religious aura, the more so as the Pope was now Napoleon's prisoner, having excommunicated the Emperor in 1809; a second Coronation along the lines of the first was out of the question, hence the need for "official literature" to generate the missing religious fervor. And who could fill the role better than Chateaubriand? But first some imperial gesture towards rapprochement was needed.

Recently, a member of the French Academy had conveniently died; perhaps Chateaubriand might fill the position and depict the Emperor in a favorable light in his acceptance speech? Chateaubriand was hesitant to allow his candidature, because traditionally, the new Immortal was then expected to extoll the virtues of his predecessor, who in this case happened to be, like Fouché, a regicide. Among the Academicians were personal enemies of

Chateaubriand, but some broad hints from the Emperor secured his election. Refusing to be compromised, Chateaubriand was most sparing in his praise; Napoleon personally censored the offensive text, which prompted the delighted author to remark that "the lion's claw has dug in everywhere, and I experienced a sort of pleasant irritation in thinking that I felt it in my side." As so often, the Emperor's fury was of brief duration, and remembering that a Caesar was expected to be forgiving towards his enemies, he appointed Chateaubriand Superintendent-General of all the libraries in France. At the same time, the Prefect of Police ordered him out of Paris—one of the recurrent inconsistencies that marked the governance of the Empire.

For some time the Napoleonic edifice had been crumbling. The war in Spain had not been resolved, and the campaign in Russia created the extraordinary conditions that alone made the bizarre Malet conspiracy possible; the wonder is not that it was based on rumor and bluff, but that it so nearly succeeded. Though Napoleon regained control of the apparatus of government, the popular uprising in Germany, climaxed by his defeat at the battle of Leipzig (October 1813), heralded the end of the Empire. With thoughts for the future, Chateaubriand set down his political ideas in his acerbic pamphlet, *De Buonaparte et des Bourbons.*

This tract was certainly the most opportunistic and effective that he ever wrote. Fact is unashamedly subordinated to exhortation and rhetoric as the sins of the Corsican Buonaparte are enumerated and the virtues of the Bourbons are contrapuntally extolled. Corruption, taxes, conscription, torture, huge losses of life, the ruin of civilization—all are the consequences of Buonaparte's misrule. Why, he is not even a good general, indifferent to suffering and hunger among his soldiers, finally deserting them in Russia. Buonaparte is callous, without a soul, an "abominable tyrant who is so lavish with French blood because he does not have a drop of this blood in his veins." Chateaubriand's indictment reaches a crescendo:

> What have you done, not with a hundred thousand, but with five million Frenchmen whom we all knew, our relatives, our friends, our brothers? This state of affairs cannot last; he has plunged us into a terrible despotism. ... What have you done for us? What do we owe to your reign? Who assassinated the duc d'Enghien, tortured Pichegru, banished Moreau, loaded the Supreme Pontiff with chains, abducted the princes of Spain, and began a blasphemous war? You! [*C'est toi!*]

By comparison, the other two parts of the diatribe are moderation itself. The Bourbons are steeped in French history and the virtues of monarchy, the descendants of a long line of enlightened kings. Louis XVIII is known for his gentleness and love of letters; he will forgive his enemies and restore France to the family of nations. Thus, the Allies must be welcomed as liberators so that once again, as in the past, may be raised the cry "which our forefathers made resound in sadness as in triumph, and which will be the signal of peace and happiness: *Vive le roi!*"

As Napoleon had not yet been unseated, such a work represented an act of great courage. Apparently, Chateaubriand kept the manuscript at night under his pillow, but during the day his terrified wife slipped it under her dress for safekeeping. One day, while crossing the Tuileries gardens, she noticed that the papers were missing, and already imagining her husband under arrest, fainted on the spot and had to be carried home. There, to her unutterable joy, she found the manuscript in its usual hiding place. In later years, Chateaubriand often repeated

Louis XVIII's declaration that the pamphlet had been worth more to him than an army of a hundred thousand men. A copy of the tract was brought to Napoleon at Fontainebleau following his first abdication; having perused it, he commented: "This part is true, that is not true. I cannot reproach Chateaubriand at all; he resisted me when I was powerful." On hearing these remarks, the recent polemicist performed a *volte-face* and acknowledged: "My admiration for Bonaparte has always been great and sincere, even when I was attacking Napoleon with most spirit." There is some consistency in this remark, for his quarrel was with the Emperor Napoleon, and not with General Bonaparte, the First Consul.

What should have been the culmination of Chateaubriand's career, the recompense for a decade dedicated to the legitimist cause, was to prove a bitter disappointment. Not only were the leading figures of the Napoleonic era allowed to retain their posts—including Talleyrand, Fouché, Fontanes, Marmont, and Ney—but, to deepen the wound, Chateaubriand found himself viewed with suspicion and virtually ignored. The Bourbons, once restored, had little use for a vigorous advocate of a free press and regarded imaginative writers with distrust. Nor had Chateaubriand's enemies forgotten his flattering dedication of the *Génie du Christianisme* to the now discredited Napoleon. His articles pleading a spirit of reconciliation were greeted indifferently, and the most he could hope for was the proffered ambassadorship to Stockholm, far removed from the center of power. Essentially a moderate constitutionalist, he sought in an article in the *Débats* to reconcile the revolutionary and the reactionary positions. The King was pleased, and even helped in the redaction of the *Réflexions politiques,* a defense of the monarchy and the liberties guaranteed in his Charter to the French people. Again, Chateaubriand's enemies ensured that his success would be temporary. He had served his purpose, and the vacillating Louis could confide to his intimates: "Beware of ever admitting a poet into your affairs; he will ruin everything. Those people are no use at all." Perhaps not; but the news of Napoleon's landing made such musings irrelevant.

Chateaubriand exhorted resistance to the invader, even if it should necessitate the King's heroic death. But Louis XVIII had little wish to emulate the more courageous among his ancestors and took the road to Belgium. If we are to believe the *Mémoires,* Chateaubriand was so disgusted at the King's cowardice that in his fury he no longer knew what he was doing and so could not prevent his wife from pushing him into a carriage at four in the morning. He soon found himself in Ghent with the Court in exile. Having gained sanctuary on foreign soil, Louis appointed Chateaubriand Minister of the Interior, a post fully in keeping with the logic of those chaotic days.

During the Hundred Days, the minister without a country continued to write in support of the Bourbon legitimacy. He knew that Talleyrand in distant Vienna was suggesting to Czar Alexander that the Duke of Orleans might make a more suitable King of France, that Fouché was secretly negotiating with Metternich's agents in Basle, while Napoleon (with the help of Benjamin Constant) was posing as the liberal statesman in Paris. Amid such intrigue and treachery, Chateaubriand saw the elderly King as the embodiment of rectitude: "that great man, now grown old, stood alone among all those traitors, men and fate, on a tottering earth, under a hostile sky, facing his performed destiny and God's judgment." Whatever his inner reservations or personal rebuffs he had suffered, Chateaubriand regarded the reestablishment of the legitimate line as his sacred duty.

The battle of Waterloo elicited one of those poetic

descriptions for which the romantic writer is noted; he was deeply moved by Napoleon's defeat and fall from power. Again, Chateaubriand could not conceal his ambivalent attitude towards his adversary who had achieved greatness, no matter how much he had abused his position. Such meditations were soon cut short by the bitter realization that once again he himself had been thrust aside by ruthless men of action; pressured by the Duke of Wellington, the King with extreme reluctance had accepted the services of Fouché and Talleyrand, one a regicide, the other an unfrocked priest. Chateaubriand had been outmaneuvered by two consummate opportunists, and had to watch in embittered silence as the loathsome pair entered to pay homage to the King:

> Suddenly a door opened: silently there entered Vice leaning on the arm of Crime, M. de Talleyrand was walking, supported by M. Fouché; the infernal vision slowly passed before me, entered the King's closet and disappeared. Fouché had just come to swear fealty and homage to his lord; the faithful regicide on his knees placed his hands, which caused the head of Louis XVI to fall, between the hands of the brother of the martyred king; the apostate bishop stood surety for the oath.

A little later the King asked Chateaubriand what he thought of the whole matter. Summoning his courage, he said: "Sire, I merely obey your orders; pardon my loyalty, but I think the monarchy is finished." After a pause, the King replied: "Well, Monsieur de Chateaubriand, I share your opinion."

The second Bourbon restoration was no happier for Chateaubriand than the first. True, his political career outwardly flourished, but somehow it was all very unsatisfactory. The last thirty years of his long life were filled with self-conscious posturing and contradictory actions. More a supporter of the legitimist monarchy as an institution or an ideal, he frequently criticized the King as an individual. Indeed, on occasion one may seriously doubt whether he believed his own utterances. As late as 1832, Chateaubriand, now a full-fledged Quixote, was seeking to place the young "Henri V" on the throne as the legitimate King of France. A letter written to Louis Napoleon, the nephew of the late Emperor, is most revealing: "You know, Prince, that my young king is in Scotland, that as long as he lives there can be no other King of France for me; but if God, in his impenetrable wisdom, were to depose the race of Saint Louis ... there is no name that better befits the glory of France than yours."

If unswerving loyalty to the principle of legitimacy was his declared lodestar, he must nevertheless have felt that it was the powerful figure of Napoleon that had captivated him. The entire third part of the *Mémoires d'Outre-Tombe*—nearly four hundred pages—is devoted to the Emperor's career; the Bourbons are passed over in relative silence. As in his own life, these impassioned pages are a monument of contradictions, of identification and rejection, of adulation and censure. Napoleon is forthrightly condemned for his shortcomings, but is it not ultimately a figure of grandeur and vision that emerges? And do we not perceive a parallel self-portrait of Chateaubriand, vain, impractical, a strutting poseur, yet curiously touching, saved by unwitting naïveté? One can only hope that poet and hero have met again beyond the tomb.

Madame de Staël

Few personalities so faithfully reflect the spirit of their age as does Germaine, Madame de Staël. In one astonishing woman may be observed the aspirations, convictions, and disappointments of a society rudely torn from its placid past and hurled into an uncertain future. If the declared purpose of the Revolution was to free mankind in general, it was equally Germaine's intention to liberate herself from the confines of society, whatever its form of government—monarchist, revolutionary, or Napoleonic. Paradoxically a voice of moderation in a tumult of violent extremes, few women have employed such passionate measures to achieve such temperate aims. Thus, all her activities, whether literary, political, or amatory, were fused into a concerted whole designed to bend others to her way of thinking. If Germaine lost most of her battles against the Emperor, she may well have won the final victory.

Though born in Paris in 1766, Germaine Necker was of Swiss Protestant background, which placed a certain distance between her and her French contemporaries. Her father, the renowned Genevan financier Jacques Necker, occupied the key position as Louis XVI's Minister of Finance, in which capacity he loaned the royal treasury two million francs. The recovery of this sum was to become an obsession with his daughter and runs throughout her life like a leitmotif until the year before her death. Germaine's attitude towards her father was divided between adulation in public and ennui at home. Largely on account of Necker's considerable fortune, Germaine was considered a good marital catch, which more than compensated for any lack of physical beauty. When she was seventeen, the possibility of an alliance with William Pitt, the son of Lord Chatham, was considered, but the future Prime Minister eluded the marital net since Germaine did not wish to be separated from her father or from Parisian society. Besides, she had fallen in love with the Swedish Count Fersen, only to discover that he in turn was in love with the Queen, Marie Antoinette.

This early disappointment was to have unhappy consequences. In contradiction to her passionate nature, she allowed herself to be married off to Fersen's companion, Eric-Magnus de Staël, seventeen years her senior. The marriage was celebrated in 1786 after considerable haggling on both sides to ensure the best possible bargain. Now twenty years old, Germaine was free from her hysterical mother, and though she never showed much affection towards her husband, and even less fidelity, she was the wife of the Swedish ambassador with entrée to the glittering society of the few remaining years of the *ancien régime*.

Later in life Germaine wrote that "the greatest happiness for a woman is to have married a man whom she respects as much as she loves, who through his mind and character is superior to her and who decides everything for her." This idealized situation certainly did not exist in her own marriage; entirely without self-discipline, vain and sensuous, she was incapable of regarding a relationship between herself and any man as based on equality, whether he be lover, political adversary or literary acquaintance. Gifted with a brilliant mind and the eloquent means to express it, she soon became the unquestioned arbiter of her salon, despite her unpopularity among rival *salonnières*. Her political philosophy was liberal, favoring a constitutional monarchy modeled after the English pattern, though taking into account French traditions and national characteristics. Throughout her life, the world of ideas and their impassioned advocacy were to overshadow the duties of wife and mother. Germaine was more interested in reforming society than in reforming herself, preferring to limit her efforts to the possible.

Having allowed her husband to father a son, Auguste, Germaine entered into liaisons with Talleyrand, then Bishop of Autun, and Louis de Narbonne, soon to become Minister of War. The *douceur de vivre* that Talleyrand so cherished under the *ancien régime* soon deteriorated into the confusion and violence of the Revolution. Mme de Staël's many connections with men in high position made it difficult for her to remain a passive bystander during the coming upheaval; her emotional character made it impossible. One rainy October day she witnessed the direct confrontation between the royal family and a crowd of infuriated women and children at Versailles. Germaine exhibited her characteristic courage, and despite her personal coolness toward the Queen, she loyally remained at her side.

With the approach of the storm, the frivolity and scandals of the salons increasingly gave way to political discussion and weightier subjects. "Never," wrote Mme de Staël in retrospect, "was society at once so brilliant and so serious as during the first three or four years of the Revolution, reckoning from 1788 to 1791." For Germaine, the fragile world of the salon soon began to crumble; that she survived the months of terror is a credit to her courage and tenacity. Paris in the summer of 1792 had lost the idealism of three years earlier. Violence and fanaticism tyrannized the city. The Swiss mercenary guard, defending the royal family at the Tuileries, was massacred by the mob. Whatever her lack of emotional control in affairs of the heart, Germaine was very practical in everyday matters and in moments of crisis. When her lover Narbonne's life was threatened, she hid him under the altar of the chapel in the Swedish embassy while alternately cajoling and threatening the guard posted outside the building. Eventually he fled to England with a false passport, but Germaine remained in Paris to help others escape the September massacres. It was only with the greatest difficulty that Mme de Staël, now seven months pregnant with Narbonne's child, avoided being hacked to pieces by an angry rabble.

Leaving the terrorized city, Germaine made her way to the family home in Coppet on the northern shore of Lake Geneva. She soon became bored with provincial life and the wearisome company of her parents. After the birth of Albert on November 20, she left for England to rejoin Narbonne and the unfrocked Talleyrand, arriving there at the same time as the news of Louis XVI's execution.

Life at Juniper Hall, a gathering place of émigrés since 1792, in Surrey, had a brilliancy of its own, presided over and dominated by the new arrival. The daytime was devoted to literary research and writing, as well as to the preparation of the spontaneous *bons mots* that were to dazzle the company in the evening. Every moment was used to the full; and even on short trips by carriage the inner glass partition had been removed so that the passengers could partake of the conversation (mainly Germaine's). Among other prim English ladies, Miss Fanny Burney was shocked to discover rampant sin among the émigré group, failing to observe that Narbonne's love for the woman who had saved his life and given birth to their son had all but burnt itself out. Despite being received by Pitt and Fox, Germaine was shrewd enough to perceive that her welcome among London society was polite at best, so reluctantly she set out for Switzerland again, meeting her husband for the first time in over a year.

Possessed of tremendous vitality, Germaine turned her energies to the rescue of several potential victims of the Terror. On a more intimate level, she was distraught by Narbonne's failure to respond positively to a deluge of emotional entreaties to rejoin her, many containing graphic threats of suicide. When the recalcitrant lover eventually obeyed his mistress's command, he discovered that the Swedish Count Ribbing had supplanted him in her affections. One day Germaine imagined, somewhat optimistically, that the two men had left the house to fight a duel over her favors, only to learn that they had enjoyed the morning together on a fishing expedition.

In September 1794 began the liaison with Benjamin Constant that was to have such a profound effect on both. For the next twenty-three years he was to intertwine his life, hopes, and emotions with a woman incapable of compromise and for whom there was no such thing as ex-membership in her amatory circle. The direct literary influence of Constant on Mme de Staël is difficult to assess, though the brilliance of his intellect and lucidity of style were no doubt positive forces. Considering his chaotic youth and emotional immaturity—not to mention his compulsive gambling and wenching—it is all the more remarkable that he had anything in common with the wife of the Swedish ambassador. At first repelled by Benjamin's unremarkable appearance, Germaine was quick to appreciate his political acumen, furthered no doubt by their common Swiss Protestant background. Unfortunately, it was Benjamin who introduced Germaine to the destructive pleasures of opium, widely used as a pain killer; her addiction to the drug did not leave her until the moment she died.

In late May of 1795, Mme de Staël deemed it safe to return to Paris. Her entry with Constant should have been a great success; her husband had persuaded Sweden to recognize the revolutionary republic, and her pamphlet *Reflections on Peace*—written with Benjamin's help —was moderate and presented the French government in a favorable light. Perhaps its reasoning was too subtle for some of the raucous deputies, who attacked the authors as being secretly friendly towards the royalists plotting against the new government. Germaine's protest was to no avail, and she was ordered to leave France within ten days on the grounds of political interference; on such occasions it was convenient to regard her as a foreigner. With Benjamin Constant in attendance, she returned to Switzerland, this being but the first of several such expulsions from the country of her birth. Meanwhile, the embryo royalist insurrection against the outgoing Convention's attempt at manipulating the elections was decisively ended with a "whiff of grapeshot"; the victorious young general was Napoleon Bonaparte.

The next year was devoted to several treatises in defense of the French Republic, written both from conviction and necessity. Government spies reported on the couple's innocuous activities to their masters in Paris; the authorities relented, and in January 1797 Benjamin and Germaine installed themselves in a country home near Paris. Her Swedish husband, valuable mainly because of his diplomatic rank, chose this inopportune moment to lose his position as ambassador, at the same time incurring considerable debts. To complicate matters, Germaine gave birth to a daughter, Albertine, on June 8, 1797, Benjamin in all probability being the father on this occasion.

The second half of the year seemed more promising. Through clever manipulation, Germaine succeeded in having Talleyrand, recently returned from exile in America, appointed Minister of Foreign Affairs. She had previously helped her lover financially, but Talleyrand was not the sort of man to repay his debts, whether of the heart or of the pocket. Germaine later evened accounts in *Delphine,* in which Talleyrand is unflatteringly depicted as Madame de Vernon.

Nor did Benjamin obtain the hoped-for government post. Nevertheless, the coup d'état of 18 Fructidor (September 4, 1797) offered hope, as it projected Germaine's confidant, Paul Barras, the most ambitious member of the Directory, into power. It is probable that both Napoleon and Germaine had advance knowledge of the intended coup; in any case, shortly afterwards they met for the first time. Germaine had already pestered the victorious general during his Italian campaign with a succession of unsolicited letters; unfortunately, they also contained some unflattering remarks that reflected on Josephine's morals. Napoleon, ignoring the effusive praise comparing him to Scipio, had considered Germaine hysterical, if not mad, and did not deign to answer her importunate adulation.

The historic encounter between those whom Germaine considered to be the greatest man and woman of the age took place on December 6, 1797. Napoleon reacted indifferently, even coldly, but Germaine refused to give up after a single skirmish. When, on a later occasion, she pointedly asked him who was the greatest woman living or dead, Napoleon replied, "the one that has produced the most children." The meeting was a disaster. An apocryphal anecdote has Germaine bursting into Napoleon's house while he was taking a bath. Upon being denied a face-to-face colloquy with the general, she boldly declared that "genius has no sex"; men and women of superior intelligence were equals. Napoleon was later to reply with a code of laws that would set back women's civil rights by over a century.

What little we know of the personal relationship between Mme de Staël and Napoleon comes from several sources, mostly of doubtful objectivity. The Emperor's recollections on St. Helena are often self-serving, and though he modified his harsh criticism in later years, he was incapable of understanding what his antagonist had striven for. Germaine's unfinished *Dix années d'exil*, fascinating in its brilliant insights, is nevertheless suspect for having been written in emotional haste, often immediately following the events related. Her *Considérations sur les principaux événements de la Révolution française*, completed in 1816 shortly before her death, errs in the other direction, and is a deliberate apologia designed to set the record straight, i.e., to defend Germaine before posterity. Both of the above sources have to be weighed against her correspondence, her actions, and the testimony of eyewitnesses. It is a formidable task involving much contradictory evidence.

According to Germaine, her assessment of Napoleon is objective and devoid of personal animosity. Though she preferred the Republic to the *ancien régime,* she was apprehensive of its tendency to degenerate into a dictatorial tyranny. Thus, she boasts that she was the first to detect such traits in the young hero:

> I sensed more quickly than others—and I am proud of it—Bonaparte's character and tyrannical intentions. The true friends of liberty, in this respect, are guided by an instinct that does not deceive them.

Is the above strictly true? Written in retrospect, surely it is placing as favorable an interpretation as possible on unfortunate events, both political and personal. At first, both Germaine and her father were enthusiastic at the prospect of Napoleon's coming to power, not least of all because he would defend property rights. Germaine soon became a close acquaintance of Napoleon's brother, Joseph, and frequently called upon him to intercede on her behalf. Despite her later altercations with the "tyrant," she remained on friendly terms with Joseph, often visiting him at his country home at Mortefontaine. Within the Bonaparte family, Joseph and Lucien were considered easy-going and readily accessible, much to Napoleon's disgust. On one occasion, Joseph tried to bring Germaine into his brother's camp by assuring her of a residence in Paris and the payment of her father's two millions. Supposedly Germaine replied: "Good God! It is not what I wish, but what I think, that is in question."

These noble sentiments were interrupted by the Republic's announced intention to "liberate" Switzerland, a project that terrified Mme de Staël. The German-speaking Bernese had long ruled over the Vaudois, but Germaine in an hour's tête-à-tête with Napoleon tried to explain that her fellow-citizens enjoyed liberty *de facto,* if not *de jure.* Napoleon listened patiently, but his mind was made up; what he failed to mention was that the Bernese treasury would also be liberated in order to finance the coming Egyptian project. Germaine scurried back to Coppet, where she was relieved and delighted by the respectful attitude of the French soldiers towards her father. Nothing was touched, but the French government made it clear that Mme de Staël would do well to remain in Switzerland.

Benjamin Constant, though Swiss by birth, had preferred to remain in Paris; in fact, now that France had annexed Geneva, he hoped to become a French citizen, mindless of the fact that he had never been a resident of that city. Hopeful of a political career in Paris, he had avoided any imbroglio either with the government or with the rising Bonaparte. In any case, he had become tired of Germaine's selfish demands and wished that her exile would become permanent. Such optimism was dashed by yet another coup d'état, the decisive 18 Brumaire (November 9, 1799) that brought General Bonaparte to power as the First Consul. Again it appears that Germaine had prior knowledge, for she returned to Paris the same evening. After some anxious moments caused by Napoleon's maladroit conduct, Lucien saved the day for his brother. Germaine hoped that past misunderstandings would now be forgotten, and that she and Benjamin, with all due modesty, would be called upon to play leading roles as France entered the new century.

Although harboring reservations at the violent collapse of representative government, Benjamin opportunistically proffered his services to the country's new ruler. In a personal interview with Bonaparte, he pledged his full support to the new régime and suggested that perhaps he might be appointed a Tribune. Thanks to a good word from Joseph, his request was granted; when the Tribunate met for the first time in January 1800, he took his place as member for the newly formed Léman department of his native Switzerland.

The hundred-member body had little effective power, and a useful clause permitting the replacement of a fifth of the Tribunes took care of potential troublemakers. In return for flattering platitudes or at least uncritical silence, the members received a salary of 15,000 francs a year; it was decreed that speeches be of brief duration and implied that the less said the better. This dictatorial directive proved too much for Germaine, who had failed to make any headway with the First Consul. A public counterattack was ordered. Suppressing grave misgivings, Benjamin dutifully obeyed, and in a courageous speech shocked his fellow Tribunes with direct criticism of the First Consul. The reaction was quick and violent; the servile press ridiculed the heretical pair in abusive terms, and Parisian society ostracized their salon. With rare spirit, Constant persisted in his attacks on the erosion of legal rights, even though he fully realized it meant the end of any career under Napoleon. In January 1802, he was relieved of his post under the replacement clause; largely due to Mme de Staël, his sinecure was at an end.

Meanwhile, Germaine had also been preoccupied with her domestic life. In 1798 she had become friendly with Juliette Récamier, the beautiful young wife of a middle-aged banker. This virginal temptress played havoc with the hearts of a whole generation; none were spared, including Lucien, Napoleon, and, in later years, poor Benjamin. Her loyalty to democratic principles and steadfast resistance to Napoleon's advances earned her his enmity and the enduring friendship of Mme de Staël. At this point, Germaine was unwillingly forced to turn her attention to an object hitherto neglected, namely, her husband. Not only had his debts steadily mounted but, in inverse proportion, his health had declined. Germaine's neglect of the invalid brought forth a caustic letter from Napoleon to his brother Joseph:

> Monsieur de Staël lives in abject misery, and his
> wife gives dinners and balls. If you continue to see her,
> would it not be proper to suggest to that woman that she
> give her husband an allowance of 2,000 francs a month?

Germaine decided to return with her ailing husband to
Coppet, one of the few recorded occasions on which she
showed him any marital affection. On the homeward
journey the unfortunate man expired at a country inn;
significantly, his tomb at Coppet has been lost to posterity.

In 1800 appeared one of Mme de Staël's most substantial works, her *Literature Considered in Relation to
Social Institutions*. The theme is comprehensive and chal-
lenging, and Germaine was optimistic that its publication
would reconcile her to Bonaparte. Unfortunately, many
of the conclusions are based more on subjective convictions than on ascertainable facts. Throughout the work
runs a didactic undercurrent, the need for virtue, liberty,
and happiness among men and nations, the striving toward perfectability. Today, the book is little read, and
certainly seems innocent enough, even naïve; but its advocacy of foreign literatures—especially its praise of
Shakespeare—coupled to her failure to mention the First
Consul was enough to earn his further displeasure. In a
period of "official literature," this latter point especially
seems to have irked Napoleon, as Germaine noted several
years later:

> Bonaparte wanted me to praise him in my writings,
> certainly not that one more eulogy would have been
> noticed in the fumes of incense surrounding him, but as
> I was definitely the only writer the French knew who
> had published books under his rule without mentioning
> his mighty existence, this annoyed him so much that he
> finally suppressed my work on Germany with incredible
> fury.

In the spring of 1800, Bonaparte passed through
Geneva before crossing the Great St. Bernard to descend

on the unsuspecting Austrian armies in northern Italy. According to Germaine, "he expressed a desire to see M. Necker, my father waited upon him, more with the hope of serving me than from any other motive." It seems that Germaine was straying somewhat from the truth; it was her father who requested the meeting to ask pardon for the speech made in the Tribunate by Constant at the behest of his unmanageable daughter. Necker was so nervous that he completely forgot to mention the repayment of his two-million-franc loan. As for Napoleon, he found the former Minister of Finance a comic figure resembling a bloated schoolteacher, but the meeting was pleasant enough on both sides.

That winter Germaine met Bonaparte for the last time. She was determined to come well-prepared; in her own words:

> . . . as I knew that he expressed himself very unfavor-
> ably about me, it struck me that he might perhaps accost
> me with some of those rude expressions which he often
> took pleasure in addressing to females, even to those who
> paid their court to him; I wrote down therefore, as they
> occurred to me, before I went to the entertainment, a
> variety of tart and piquant replies which I might make
> to what I supposed he might say to me.

Regrettably, he was inconsiderate enough to ask questions that did not suit the answers; when asked whether she had nursed her children herself, Germaine was at a loss for words—a unique occasion in her life. In her memoirs, Germaine had a convenient lapse of memory regarding the above incident, merely noting that "he only addressed the most common questions possible to me." No doubt she would have preferred to discuss the proposed Concordat with the First Consul. For a brief period Germaine had hoped that Protestantism might be introduced as the state religion, and it seems that Bonaparte quite independently had considered the possibility before rejecting it as totally impractical. The Concordat was not only in keeping with French religious traditions, but offered political advantages besides; in Germaine's words, "tomorrow the tyrant will have 40,000 priests in his service." As she shrewdly foresaw, the proclamation of the Concordat was but a steppingstone to loftier ambitions.

The exact details of the Generals' Plot aimed at overthrowing Bonaparte are not clear. Mme de Staël was almost certainly involved, perhaps Fouché, and a dozen of the Republic's most famous generals. The scheme collapsed, and the First Consul, both relieved and embarrassed, exercised leniency; Germaine was merely warned to keep her distance and stay in Switzerland. On August 2, 1802, Bonaparte was made First Consul for life following the usual plebiscite. In this same year, Germaine was to suffer three further setbacks. Her father, in an optimistic moment, sent Bonaparte a copy of his *Last Views on Politics and Finance Offered to the French Nation by M. Necker* in the fond hope that somehow it might work to his daughter's advantage. The implied criticism that the new constitution rested on military power and little else infuriated the man it was supposed to mollify. The publication of Germaine's novel *Delphine* was equally unfortunate, being directed at the "silent but enlightened France." Nor was her emphasis upon the injustices meted out by men towards women superior to them in compassion and ability calculated to please. Germaine was viciously attacked in the submissive press, and Bonaparte reaffirmed his decree that she not return to Paris. The winter of 1802-03 was spent in bitter arguments with Benjamin, the temperamental Necker acting as ineffectual arbiter.

Every effort was made to have the ban revoked; Necker wrote a personal letter to Bonaparte, while Germaine in a pathetic plea to *"cher* Joseph" gave her word that "if the Consul allows me to return to France, I feel myself bound by honor not to say a word, not to write a line, not to take a step that might displease him." No mention of this letter is in her memoirs; in any case, its purpose failed. A new stratagem was required, and Benjamin was given his conditional freedom provided that he buy a house near Paris. Far from acting the role of Trojan Horse on behalf of Germaine, he had plans for escape and even matrimony. What he did not know was that Germaine had received a partial reprieve, allowing her to settle at a distance of ten leagues from Paris. Benjamin's domestic reveries were rudely disrupted by the sudden descent of his former custodian; every effort was now concentrated on getting Germaine within the walls of the city.

The first assault was directed against Bonaparte himself in two emotional letters that attempted to cajole her tormentor into unintended concessions. Using the education of her children as a pretext, she gave further assurances that her conduct would be exemplary. Bonaparte ignored each successive plea; he had heard reports that Mme de Staël's residence at Mafliers had become the center of various groups hostile to the Consulate. His reaction was swift; Germaine wrote:

> ... Bonaparte immediately seized the pretext, or the motive that was given him to banish me, and I was informed by one of my friends that a gendarme would be with me in a few days with an order for me to depart. One has no idea in countries where routine at least secures individuals from any act of injustice of the terror which the sudden news of arbitrary acts of this nature inspires.

Joseph and Lucien were implored to intercede once again, and Juliette Récamier—already in a precarious position —and General Junot added their voices on Germaine's behalf. The First Consul remained adamant, and on October 13 signed a decree ordering her to remove herself to a distance of forty leagues from Paris; she was to leave within twenty-four hours. As luck would have it, the gendarme designated to bring Mme de Staël the order was one of her admirers, and risking his master's wrath, allowed her to spend three days in Paris in order to straighten out her late husband's financial affairs. A considerate invitation from Joseph to be his guest at Mortefontaine offered a glimmer of hope, but his brother remained implacable. Very well, if exiled from Paris and her friends, she would conquer new territories further afield. Packing her children and Benjamin into a carriage, Germaine headed east towards Germany, at that time *terra incognita* to most Frenchmen.

Germaine visualized her projected journey as a rebuff to Bonaparte, an imperial progress that would confirm her position as the most brilliant woman of her age. At Weimar she met both Goethe and Schiller, not as an humble pilgrim visiting a literary shrine, but rather as an equal ready to do intellectual battle. Whatever was lacking in her command of German—fortunately for her, French was still the principal cultural language—was more than compensated for by her energy and self-confidence. To a visiting Englishman she modestly confided that "whatever I don't understand is nothing," which greatly simplified any discussion. It was therefore most disconcerting to observe that Benjamin (who spoke fluent German) had made by far the more favorable impression on the two resident Olympians. She was not unhappy to continue alone to Berlin where she succeeded in ensnaring the great scholar and linguist, August Wilhelm Schlegel, ostensibly as cultural adviser and her children's tutor.

Meanwhile, Benjamin had returned to Lausanne, where he learned of the death of Necker; immediately he left for Germany to break the news to Germaine. Deeply shaken at the loss of her father, she now found herself in sole charge of the court at Coppet. The following years witnessed some of the most brilliant gatherings ever assembled at what Stendhal later described as "the States-General of European opinion." Having failed to soften Napoleon's heart, Mme de Staël was determined to make Coppet the intellectual Mecca of the continent; if the Emperor (as he now was) refused to allow her access to Paris, Paris would have to come to her on the shores of Lake Geneva. Here Germaine ruled supreme, presiding over an admiring audience of literati including the historian Sismondi, Bonstetten, the naturalist, and a penitent Benjamin. The most welcome visitor was Juliette Récamier, whose dislike of Napoleon became even further pronounced after his insulting remarks on the occasion of her husband's bankruptcy in 1805. Declaring that he "was not Madame Récamier's lover"—not for want of trying—he refused to permit the banker a loan that would have averted the catastrophe. What he could not have foreseen was the surge of sympathy extended to the Récamiers, who were widely regarded as victims of oppression.

During the first half of 1805 Germaine undertook a long-contemplated journey to Italy, crossing the Alps with Schlegel and her three children. No doubt she was disappointed that the Emperor had not granted her an imperial pardon at the time of his Coronation; a second chance might present itself in Milan during the festivities to mark Napoleon's acceptance of the Italian crown. But, perhaps fearing a further rebuff, Germaine avoided another confrontation and traveled to Rome and Naples, finding solace in a passionate affair with a young Portuguese nobleman while gathering impressions for another novel. In June the travel party was back at Coppet for a summer devoted to theatrical productions, writing, and furious domestic squabbles. Germaine ruled as literary empress, issuing imperious commands with a green branch to her guests assembled around the table. It was she who decided whether the topic for discussion would be political, cultural, or merely amusing, or whether a scene was to be declaimed from some classical tragedy. Whatever the selection, the dominant voice was that of the chatelaine who fascinated her audience with inspired improvisations, often laboriously composed during the earlier part of the day. Notwithstanding her theatrical posturing and such witticisms as Byron's quip that "she thought like a man, but alas! she felt like a woman," her mind was one of the most incisive of a brilliant age. It is to Mme de Staël that we owe much of our understanding of the period.

Coppet, however, was far from being Paris. Germaine had not been exiled from France entirely, and was allowed to travel freely provided she did not transgress an invisible circle radiating forty leagues (just under 120 miles) from the capital. In the spring of 1806 she established her entourage first in Auxerre and then, more daringly, in Rouen. Her two sons were sent on to Paris in the care of Schlegel, who also was used as a front man in the purchase of some property. Fouché's spies followed every move, and transcriptions of Germaine's correspondence were forwarded to the Emperor in distant Prussia. The Minister of Police and Mme de Staël respected the ability and character of one another; besides, both hoped that Napoleon would be decisively defeated. Accordingly, when Germaine slipped into Paris under cover of dark, Fouché was quite prepared to turn a blind eye, this despite direct orders from the Emperor in Poland "not to let that hussy get close to Paris." The imperial anger and language were extreme when the facts were reported. Fulminating at his minister, he included the contents of an intercepted letter, adding, "You can

see from this letter what a good Frenchwoman we have
here. . . . I shall not tell you what plans this ridiculous
group has made in the happy event that I should be killed,
since one can assume that a Minister of Police knows all
about this." An embarrassed Fouché was given the dates
of Germaine's stay in Paris and told that "this whore"
was to be restricted to Coppet. A six-page letter from
Germaine to the Emperor was received with derision, as
was a copy of her novel *Corinne*. There was little choice
for her but to retreat to the sanctuary of Coppet and to
prepare for the summer season.

The following months at the château were of an as-
tounding brilliance. In an international ambiance, everyone worked, conversed, and wrote; no doors were locked,
and as many as thirty guests and fifteen servants jostled
one another democratically under the watchful eye of
their hostess. Plays were performed in the library, and
guests were encouraged to act minor parts in support of
Germaine, Juliette, and Benjamin, who took the main
roles. Bonstetten could claim—with some exaggeration—
that "more witty things are said at Coppet in one day
than in one year throughout the rest of the world." Despite the oratory, coquetry, and the usual emotionally-
charged arguments, the Emperor had not been forgotten.
Mindful of her own failures that winter, Germaine sent
her elder son, Auguste, to petition Napoleon on her behalf. The young man courageously presented his mother's
case, the Emperor was in a relaxed mood, but nothing
came of it; Mme de Staël was a foreigner—Swiss?
Swedish?—so why was she so anxious to live in Paris
under his tyranny? Germaine seems to have anticipated
a negative reply, for at that moment she was about to
reach Vienna with the dutiful Schlegel.

The five-month stay in the Austrian capital is now
mainly remembered for Schlegel's famous series of lectures on dramatic literature. Other than yet another ro-

mantic entanglement, Germaine apparently contented herself with the active social life occasioned by the third
marriage of Francis I, the Emperor of Austria and the
future father-in-law of Napoleon. Though she attended
several concerts, it would appear that she was unaware
of, or had little interest in, the revolution that music was
undergoing in Beethoven's compositions. As usual, her
activities were followed by a bevy of spies, both French
and Austrian, and by late spring she was glad to set out
on the homeward journey, returning through southern
Germany. Apparently she made contact with a group of
allegedly anti-French conspirators; the incident is unclear,
but Napoleon, who was in Bayonne supervising the abdication *en masse* of the Spanish Bourbons, ordered her
surveyed by his secret police. Germaine stayed a few
days in Weimar, despite Goethe's absence; incredibly, the
German sage regarded Napoleon more important than
"Our Lady of Coppet," as Constant's cousin referred to
her.

Upon her return she discovered that Benjamin had
committed the most heinous of crimes—he had married
in secret without his captor's permission. Once again, the
very ground erupted, but increasingly her energies were
concentrated on the writing of *De l'Allemagne,* the gene-
sis of which went back several years. Schlegel's role in
the creation of the work is uncertain, probably more dis-
cernible in the basic preparation than in its final form.
The style and observations—notably the final chapter on
religion and enthusiasm—reveal the essence of Germaine's
thought in every sentence, and, given her independence
of character, it could hardly have been otherwise. When
finally published, the book introduced Frenchmen to the
culture of their neighbors and helped disseminate German
romanticism. It is easy to criticize the work; it is often
inaccurate, and the subjective judgments faulty for want
of supporting evidence. Though badly dated and little

read today—at least not as a source of reliable information—*De l'Allemagne* still remains a literary watershed. That it was published at all was a major achievement.

Having nearly completed the manuscript, Germaine established her court at the castle of Chaumont-sur-Loire so as to be close to both publisher and printer. The summer of 1810 nearly matched those of Coppet in its wit and verve; only the replacement of the accommodating Fouché by General Savary as Minister of Police cast a shadow that was to increase in length. Germaine had taken great pains to submit her work to the censor, and the marriage of the Emperor to a German-speaking princess was regarded as a favorable omen. The book was already in print when the blow descended; all copies were ordered destroyed by Savary, and Germaine once again was exiled. Her father had bought considerable property in the United States, and on receiving the terrible news, Germaine seriously considered crossing the Atlantic. Fortunately, her son Auguste had retained a copy of the manuscript, but in spite of the usual pathetic pleas to the Emperor, there was no course of action possible other than the voyage to America or enforced retreat to Coppet. After a brief hesitation, she chose the latter.

What had caused this latest fiasco? Again, her chief crime was that of praising foreign cultures and, by inference, criticizing France. In a letter addressed to her, Savary admitted as much:

> It has appeared to me that the air of this country did not at all agree with you, and we are not yet reduced to seek models in the nations you admire. Your last work is un-French; it is on my orders that the printing was stopped. I regret the loss your publisher will suffer, but I cannot allow it to appear.

Another fear was that the positive remarks would give the Germans renewed confidence in themselves even after successive defeats. Goethe, an arch-conservative in political matters, used the above argument as late as February 1814 to defend his view that "the French police . . . have wisely reduced it [the book] to pulp."

Though outwardly still buoyant, Germaine in fact was entering the autumn of her life. Now restricted to a distance of two leagues from Coppet, she was a virtual prisoner in her own home, spied upon even by her servants. The new prefect of Geneva suggested that she write a flattering verse to the Emperor to celebrate the birth of his son; Germaine gently rejected the idea, confining herself to the wish that the infant have a good nurse. In great secret, she had met and fallen in love with a twenty-three-year-old veteran of the Spanish war. Jean Rocca was frail in physique and certainly no intellectual match for his mistress, nearly twice his age; nevertheless, he remained loyal to Germaine to the end, apparently deeply in love with her. From this union was born the retarded child affectionately called "Petit Nous" who, in a more practical if less tender moment, was farmed out to a pastor's family.

On May 22, 1812, Germaine managed to avoid the attention of Napoleon's secret police and leave Coppet, thanks largely to Schlegel's having acquired the necessary documents:

> In this manner, after ten years of continually increasing persecutions, first sent away from Paris, then banished into Switzerland, afterwards confined to my own château, and at last condemned to the dreadful punishment of never seeing my friends, and of being the cause of their banishment: in this manner I was obliged to leave, as a fugitive, two countries, France and Switzerland, by order of a man less French than myself: for I was born on the banks of that Seine where his tyranny alone naturalizes him.

Despite the military preparations for the Russian campaign of that year, Germaine began her circuitous journey across Europe, traveling through a large part of the Austro-Hungarian Empire and the Ukraine on her way to St. Petersburg and Stockholm. With her daughter, Schlegel, and Rocca, she reached Moscow, the "Asian Rome," a few weeks before Napoleon's armies; her impression of Czar Alexander was most favorable, praising his sincerity and interest in the welfare of his people. In Stockholm she persuaded her old friend Bernadotte, now the Swedish Crown Prince, to take up arms against Napoleon, his former Emperor, hinting that he might become ruler in France (in one optimistic moment Germaine even considered the possibility that somehow she might be called upon to become Queen!).

The next few months in London were marked by the literary success of the publication of *De l'Allemagne*. Her social triumph was saddened doubly by the news of the death of Narbonne, one of her more significant loves, and that of her younger son Albert, senselessly killed in a duel of his own making. Germaine put on a bold front, launching into a swirl of social life that amazed everyone, including Byron. Her animated political discussions were an unconvincing means to disguise an inner weariness, and even the news of Napoleon's fall, which enabled her to return to her beloved Paris, did little to revive her spirits.

On May 12, 1814—nearly two years after her flight from Coppet—Mme de Staël was back in the city from which she had been exiled for so many years. Though she met many of her acquaintances again, the old drive was no longer there. Germaine barely had enough time to become disenchanted with the restored Bourbon monarchy when news of Napoleon's flight from Elba reached the French capital. She had always remained on excellent terms with his brother Joseph, but now began to think more kindly of the Emperor as well, going so far as to

warn him of an attempt against his life. The failure of
the Hundred Days soon made any personal feelings irrelevant, and even the later return of the two million francs
her father had loaned the French government a quarter
of a century previously was more for the benefit of her
daughter than for herself.

Greatly saddened by the spectacle of foreign troops
occupying Paris, she felt that no true French-born sovereign would have reduced this most civilized of cities to
such an indignity. In wishing the downfall of the tyrant,
she had given little thought as to how this might be ac-
complished. Perhaps, like Chateaubriand, she had secretly
hoped that the French armies would be victorious at
Waterloo but that Napoleon might have fallen on the
field of battle. Such a heroic death would also have resolved her ambivalent feelings towards the only man she
ever acknowledged her equal.

Her secret marriage to Rocca in 1816 was little more
than the union of two invalids sharing their last months
on earth together; the years of opium had finally taken
their toll. Summoning her last energies, Germaine left
Coppet, where she had remained following Napoleon's
second abdication, and returned to Paris. Now fifty years
old, but suffering illnesses that beset the elderly—a cere-
bral stroke and paralysis in the legs—she embraced a
personal mysticism as the end approached. One of her
last visitors was Chateaubriand, "dear Francis," who renewed a nearly-forgotten friendship with Juliette Récamier, thanks to Germaine's thoughtful invitation. Perhaps she suspected what the future would bring as she
returned to her sickroom, leaving the two together. Death
finally came on July 14, 1817—Bastille Day—to be followed by her final journey to Coppet, where she lies
buried in the family vault.

In her work on the French Revolution, written the year before she died, Mme de Staël cast many a retrospective glance towards Napoleon. She knew that she had struggled with no ordinary mortal but with a figure of extraordinary dimensions:

> I noticed quickly enough on the different occasions I had of meeting him during my stay in Paris that his character could not be delineated by using the words we are accustomed to; he was neither good, nor violent, neither pleasant nor cruel in the way individuals are whom we know. Such a being, having nothing in common with others, could neither feel nor make felt, any human warmth; he was both more and less than a man.

Four years later, the ex-Emperor died, as he had been born, on an island. He had felt the loneliness of exile, the same fate to which he had condemned so many of his adversaries. During his solitary walks he must have ruminated on his treatment of the most eminent woman of the age. What if he had listened to her advice instead of driving her into opposition? Could he, the Emperor, have deigned to accept the counsel of a woman? Why did she refuse to compromise when they had so much in common? The questions, like the ocean around St. Helena, are endless.

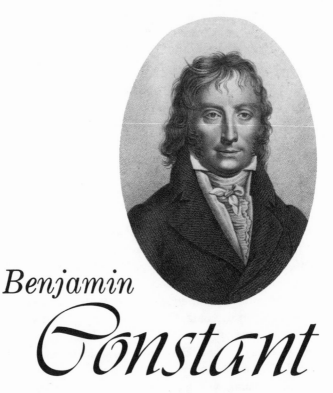

Benjamin Constant

On September 26, 1794, a young horseman of unprepossessing appearance could be seen galloping after an ornate carriage as it lumbered along the dusty road that followed the northern shore of the Lake of Geneva. Having bidden the coachman rein in the horses, the rider courteously requested the occupant's permission to accompany her on the remainder of her journey. We are acquainted with the lady, Germaine, Madame de Staël, already the most illustrious woman in Europe; her new travel companion was Benjamin Constant, at that time an obscure figure, totally unknown, and rightly so.

Benjamin Constant de Rebecque was born in Lausanne in 1767 of old Huguenot aristocracy. Following the original expulsion from France, the family with Calvinist assiduity had acquired several properties in the canton of Vaud. The sudden decline in the family's fortunes was directly attributable to the unbalanced character of Benjamin's father, Colonel Juste de Constant. Like many Vaudois, he bitterly resented the suzerainty of Berne over his homeland, and in keeping with ancient Swiss tradition sought military service abroad. In this unstable milieu, his sensitive son grew up bedeviled with ingrained feeling of perplexity and inadequacy which assailed him throughout life.

Most of what we know about Benjamin's youth comes from his own candid pen. The *Cahier rouge* is a picaresque account of the first twenty years of his life, an extended confessional of a wasted youth. His education was placed in the hands of a succession of ill-chosen tutors selected after the minimum of enquiry, some adept at reinforcing their deficient pedagogy with liberal thrashings (so much for the theories of Rousseau and Pestalozzi in their native Switzerland). When Benjamin was thirteen, his father enrolled him at Oxford, a disastrous experiment that ended, as usual, with another tutor. Later he was successively packed off to the universities of Erlangen (where he became proficient in German, gambling, and making a fool of himself) and Edinburgh (where he learned English with a Scottish brogue, gambled more, but also acquired the valuable art of public speaking). Edinburgh was an outstanding center of learning, yet even in the company of distinguished scholars, he was impressive with his skills as a writer and orator. Just as important, he came to appreciate not only the theory but also the practice of parliamentary institutions. The eighteen months in the Scottish capital provided him with the accomplishments that throughout life stood in strange juxtaposition with his irresponsible behavior.

The next few years followed the same desultory pattern. Besides a prodigious amount of unrelated knowledge, he acquired a classical conciseness of language that enabled him to expound his ideas with an assertiveness frequently lacking in his character. He expressed his liberal turn of mind with an eloquence and sincerity that helped disguise his innate shyness. These attributes were unhappily counterbalanced by his passion for gambling, a feeling that life was little more than a game of faro; to this must be added an addiction to opium, his inveterate wenching, and inability to sustain a deeper emotional experience.

An early fiasco was his courtship of a banker's attractive daughter. Faced with an embarrassing situation during a family meeting, Benjamin decided that he had sufficient audience for a dramatic performance, and after a grandiloquent speech in which he bade farewell to life, swallowed a phial of opium, taking good care that most was spilt. This "suicide" attempt, soon to become the romantic fashion throughout Europe, was, of course, an act of self-dramatization; like the many others later in life, it was followed by the same miraculous recovery. By his own admission, the whole incident was contrived, and a few minutes later everyone—including our Werther *manqué*—was dressed to attend the opera.

In quick succession there followed a madcap gallop through England and Scotland with further disreputable adventures in several countries. In desperation his father procured a ceremonial post for his wayward son at the provincial court in Brunswick in northern Germany. Benjamin surpassed all previous stupidities by rushing into marriage with a woman seven years his senior, neither attractive nor wealthy, with whom he had practically nothing in common. The outbreak of the French Revolution and the arrival of the émigrés who sought refuge in Brunswick helped divert his attention from increasing marital problems; he found additional solace in a two-month affair with Charlotte von Marenholtz, a young married lady of the local aristocracy, who was good-natured and quite willing to change husbands. Typically, Benjamin procrastinated, even though his own marriage was finished (the final divorce came in 1795). Instead, he waited fourteen years—not to be the most tranquil of his life—before marrying the woman who understood him so well.

Benjamin returned to Switzerland a failure. He had little to show for his twenty-seven years; his emotional and immature behavior belied an incisive mind and a biting wit oddly combined with great sensitivity. In the first few weeks after their meeting, Mme de Staël found little appealing about her new admirer. Though she appreciated his keen intellect and shared his liberal views on religion and politics, his pasty complexion and lack of aristocratic bearing repelled her. Not only was she still enamoured of Count Ribbing, but she was disgusted by Benjamin's maladroit declarations of love, which appeared juvenile in contrast with the sophisticated approach of her established lovers.

One night the whole household was awakened by the piercing cries of Benjamin, who had taken poison to prove his eternal love for his disdainful mistress and was now writhing in what was surely his final agony. Germaine was quickly summoned to the moribund's bedside, whereupon the expiring lover exclaimed, "Ah, it is you! You are restoring me to life!" At once assessing the situation, Germaine in an imperious voice told him to put a stop to the nonsense. "Ah, as you order it, I will try to live," he sighed. To no one's surprise, Benjamin's recovery was both rapid and complete. Perhaps more remarkable was his success in supplanting his rivals in Germaine's affections once she had overcome her initial aversion. Presumably they became lovers in April of 1795, but of

greater importance was her choice of Benjamin to accompany her to Paris that summer.

The bond that held them together was not primarily
physical, though probably Benjamin was the father of her
daughter Albertine, born two years later. Both were cosmopolitan and liberal by conviction, and passionately involved in literature and politics. Furthermore, they shared
a dislike of the provincialism of Swiss life and yearned
for the vibrancy of Paris. In character they complemented
one another, accepting a relationship that thrived on
friction and mutual hostility. Above all, they delighted in
the thrust and counterthrust of lively conversation, the
exercise of wit and imagination, the intoxication of rais-
ing language to new heights. The negative side is all too
apparent: while Germaine aroused Benjamin from his
frequent acedia, she willfully undermined his self-esteem
and independence of thought and action, retarding his
political career for nearly twenty years. The final ignominy was a state of mental bondage imposed by Biondetta,
as Benjamin was wont to call his jailor. Far from liberat-
ing his genius, she placed it in servitude.

In May 1795, Constant and Mme de Staël crossed the
border into France with much trepidation, arriving in
Paris nine days later to an unenthusiastic reception.
Though Benjamin was ineligible under the new Constitution to run for office until the age of thirty—he was now
twenty-eight—and the question of his eligibility for
French nationality remained unresolved, nevertheless
Germaine was determined to thrust her protégé into
politics. His first venture into the field of pamphleteering
was disastrous, resulting in a hasty repudiation of his
first tract once it became clear that he had misjudged
the newly proposed electoral law. Despite their advocacy
of a moderate course, the recent arrivals were widely re-

garded as foreign intriguers, and the subsequent decree ordering them to leave the country was greeted with general acclaim. This first sally into the maelstrom of postrevolutionary politics ended with the return to Coppet on Christmas Day.

Constant now saw himself the prisoner of an insoluble paradox; he needed Mme de Staël's influence and support to further his career, yet at the same time she represented the main barrier to success. In his later novel *Adolphe,* the Baron T— tells the protagonist, a thinly-disguised Benjamin: "Every road is open to you: letters, arms, administration; you can aspire to the most illustrious matches; you can succeed in anything you like: but remember that, between you and all forms of success, there is one insurmountable obstacle—and that obstacle is Ellénore [Germaine]." During the next few years Benjamin made numerous half-hearted attempts at unraveling this Gordian knot of his own making.

Practically the whole of 1796 was spent in feverish literary activity at Coppet. Though under the constant surveillance of French spies, in their writings the pair strongly supported the new Directory and the Constitution. Benjamin's pamphlet *On the Strength of the Present Government and on the Need to Support It* is a cogent defense of civil rights and established law in the face of arbitrary changes. This consistent position in all of his tracts is a partial apology for the author's subsequent shifting maneuvers; political figures are but temporary, and therefore replaceable, whereas principles and law are basic to any viable society. The Directory was so impressed by the force of his argument that the article was published in its entirety in the *Moniteur.* Unfortunately, though praising Constant's contribution, the Directory also pointed out that he still remained a foreigner as his father had failed to take advantage of a law that enabled those of Huguenot background to regain French nationality.

Yet all hopes for any future in Paris rested with Benjamin, who had received permission to return. As a permanent residence was deemed essential to apply for French nationality and to launch a political career, he obtained a loan of 34,000 francs from Germaine's father with which he bought a property in Hérivaux, some twenty miles north of the capital. Germaine cautiously joined him later, giving birth to Albertine in early June of 1797. Benjamin was the putative father, and to his credit developed a lasting affection towards the child.

Despite the publication of further pamphlets, Constant's political progress failed to match Mme de Staël's aspirations. Once again they misjudged the prevailing sentiment, believing that the country was prepared for a constitutional monarchy on the English pattern in which "the King reigns, but does not govern." This hope was dashed by the coup d'état of 18 Fructidor (September 4, 1797) instigated by Barras, which destroyed the royalist position. The move came as no surprise, as Barras was on friendly terms with Germaine; nevertheless, the character of the coup and the subsequent reprisals were distasteful to moderates. Germaine helped as many as possible escape deportation, but Benjamin perceived that his earlier enthusiasm for Barras had, in effect, unwittingly lent his support to what was clearly an illegal action. As a somewhat cynical reward, he received the meaningless title of President of the Canton of Luzarches.

Meanwhile, the French had occupied and annexed the greater part of French-speaking Switzerland which, notwithstanding the humiliation, at least opened the way to Benjamin's becoming a French citizen. Now thirty, he twice presented himself to the electors as a candidate for the Council of Five Hundred, failing on both occasions. Having played for the highest stakes and lost, he consoled himself with the usual gaming and wenching.

Already a definite change had occurred in the attitude between the two lovers. The short-lived physical attraction was at an end, and an increasing hostility had become apparent. The deterioration of the liaison was briefly halted by Bonaparte's accession to power through the coup d'état of 18-19 Brumaire (November 9-10, 1799). The new Constitution—the usual device under the Republic to legitimatize a coup—created the impressive façade of a Senate, a Tribunate, a Legislative Body, and a Council of State, imposing assemblies requiring numerous appointments. Napoleon regarded Constant as an extension of Mme de Staël and was at first loath to consider him for office, aware, no doubt, of his strong constitutional convictions. As he recalled many years later on St. Helena, "Joseph pestered me to have Benjamin Constant nominated to the Tribunate ... finally I gave in," but in fact it was a direct conversation between the two men that allayed Bonaparte's worst fears.

Benjamin now imagined himself Head of the Loyal Opposition *à l'anglaise*; Bonaparte felt that by paying him a salary of 15,000 francs a year he should regard silence as golden. The next day, in a speech that reverberated through the startled Tribunate, Constant, under Mme de Staël's influence, protested the lack of free expression. It was a courageous gesture, but futile; at the first opportunity Bonaparte dismissed him. "He should have known that I do not buy my enemies; I stamp on them," was Napoleon's later summary of the incident. Benjamin's temerity cost him dearly. It was only in 1815 that he returned to an active role in politics, ironically to serve Napoleon during the Hundred Days.

Seeing his embryonic political career destroyed, Benjamin sought refuge from Germaine's insistent demands in the company of Julie Talma and Anna Lindsay. Julie's husband, the greatest actor of the day and a favorite of Napoleon, had deserted her, and her health had begun to deteriorate. The unselfish love of these two women was later to form the framework of his semiautobiographical novel, *Adolphe,* but Benjamin preferred to analyze their relationship in detached fashion rather than accept the responsibilities of marriage to Anna. In any case, the arrival of Germaine, who had failed in her clumsy efforts at reconciliation with Bonaparte, put an end to the matter. Benjamin's subjugation to Germaine was such that, shortly after the death of her husband in 1802, he imagined it his duty to propose marriage to the widow; much to his relief, he was rejected out of hand.

Fondly imagining that he had obtained his release, Benjamin bought a small cottage a short distance from Paris, assuming that safe from Biondetta he could concentrate on finding a suitable wife, perhaps even salvaging his political career. He tried not to identify himself too closely with the idealogues so thoroughly despised by Bonaparte, and there is considerable evidence that, left to himself, he would have made his peace with the Consulate. Both his domestic and political reveries were rudely interrupted by the sudden descent of Germaine, who had come to lay siege to Paris, from which she was still barred. Bonaparte withstood the onslaught, decreeing banishment from the capital and environs; Germaine was forced to retreat, but only after exacting a promise from a recalcitrant Benjamin to follow her to Germany.

It was Constant's diplomatic presence that prevented the meeting with Goethe and Schiller at Weimar from ending disastrously. Schiller's French was hesitant, whereas Constant had become fluent in German during his years in Brunswick. Language, however, was not the main problem; Mme de Staël criticized freely, to the point of rudeness, so that her departure after two months —an eternity, the Germans must have felt—was not protested. Benjamin's brief reprieve in Lausanne was shattered by the death of Necker. Misfortune, far from promising freedom, chained the two closer together. The *Journal intime,* which dates from this period (1803), reveals Constant's increasing mental anguish and frustration, a daily confessional foreboding impending crisis. The only surprise is that the *dénouement* was not played out earlier.

Germaine's journey to Italy in 1805 gave Benjamin a rare opportunity to act on his own. Here was his chance to escape—he must marry, but whom? Characteristically, rather than create his own opportunities, he preferred Fate to decide matters for him. Ever since leaving the court at Brunswick he had carried on a sporadic correspondence with Charlotte, mainly on her initiative. She was now married to her second husband but expressed her willingness to leave him. With a decision forced upon him, Benjamin resorted to evasive introspection. This time there was a difference; out of his turmoil came *Adolphe,* perhaps the greatest psychological novel of the early romantic period.

Somewhat foolishly, Benjamin allowed Germaine to peruse the manuscript. Ignoring the author's defensive remark that "Ellénore was not a woman of exceptional intelligence," Germaine had no hesitation identifying herself with the sacrifices and suffering of the heroine. Besides, what other woman could there be in Benjamin's life? It was only after a second reading that she was assailed by the suspicion that something was wrong, resulting in a frenzy that lasted two days and caused poor Benjamin to cough up blood. Ellénore, in fact, is a composite figure, a synthesis of Anna Lindsay, Julie Talma, Charlotte, and—in the more emotional scenes—Mme de

Staël. Adolphe in vain longs for a wife and a final break with Ellénore: "What! I can't be free for a single day! I cannot breathe one hour in peace! She pursues me everywhere, like a slave who must be brought back to her feet." The "athlete shackled at the bottom of a cell" is unmistakably Benjamin; his jailor is equally recognizable as Biondetta.

Artistic life at Coppet reached its fullest expression during the summer of 1807. The season's apogee was a presentation of Racine's *Andromaque* in which Germaine played the powerful role of Hermione opposite the timid Pyrrhus of Benjamin. The latter is murdered at Hermione's command for having dared fall in love with another, a threat that an abject Benjamin had to endure in public. The humiliating performance over, Benjamin summoned his courage and delivered an ultimatum: Biondetta must either marry him or release him. In a theatrical gesture, Germaine, gathering her children and Schlegel, pointed to the presumptuous Benjamin and told them: "There's the man who places me between despair and the need to compromise your existence and fortune!" At this, the recent Pyrrhus coldly informed his Hermione that he would never marry her, whereupon she terrified those present with a harrowing attempt at self-strangulation with a shawl, fully worthy of any of Benjamin's past efforts. The following day he sought refuge at his cousin Rosalie's, to no avail; soon piercing screams were heard below, and upon investigation Germaine was found lying on the staircase, bare-bosomed and raving, "Where is he? I've got to find him!" Benjamin foolishly revealed his hiding place, and amid reproaches and curses was marched back into captivity.

Together with Schlegel, Mme de Staël traveled to Vienna in the spring of 1808, whereupon Benjamin timorously rejoined Charlotte. Finally the two were married, only to receive word that Germaine was on her way back to Coppet. The conditioning of fourteen years was not easily shrugged off; the marriage was to be kept a sworn secret until Mme de Staël could be informed at an opportune moment. Like a truant schoolboy summoned by his headmistress, Benjamin made his servile way back to Coppet, but when the opportunity arose to break the news to his enslaver, his courage failed him completely. It was left to Charlotte the following spring to inform Mme de Staël of the terrible truth. In a scene of volcanic intensity lasting six hours, Germaine screamed that Benjamin was hers and that the marriage was invalid; upon regaining her composure somewhat, she insisted that public disclosure of the whole matter be hushed up and that Benjamin return to her as soon as possible.

The summer of 1810 proved to be the turning point. While Mme de Staël was putting the finishing touches to *De l'Allemagne*—apparently her mastery of the spoken word did not extend to the subtleties of written French, and on occasion Benjamin was called upon for discreet repair work—he was dealt one of his luckier hands. Quite unexpectedly, Germaine secretly agreed to marry the young war hero, Jean Rocca. Due to a misunderstanding, Constant and Rocca nearly fought a duel over her affections, but Germaine intervened to prevent farce from becoming tragedy. The leave-taking took place in the staircase of the Hôtel de la Couronne in Lausanne on May 8, 1811, at midmorning; though Benjamin and Germaine were to meet again in Paris three years later, this in effect was the final adieu. "I believe we shall never see one another again," she said, to which he replied: "We shall never really be separated from one another." Factually, neither statement was correct, yet in a deeper sense both spoke the truth.

Finally free of his tormentor, Benjamin left with Charlotte for her family home in Germany. Since his dismissal from the Tribunate, he had watched Napoleon's star rise and fall. The declining military fortunes of the Emperor, graphically described to him by Narbonne on his return from Russia in 1813, reawakened political ambitions long dormant. Shortly after the battle of Leipzig, in his *On the Spirit of Conquest and on Usurpation with Respect to European Civilization* (Constant's titles are as windy as his style is concise) he stated a truth valid for all times:

> Certain governments, when they send their legions from one pole to the other, still talk about the defense of their hearths; one could say that they call their hearths every place to which they have set fire.

War and dictators were anachronisms in a civilized world of commerce; militarism was based on lies and imposed uniformity on all men.

The tract is not merely a fulminating condemnation of Napoleon; rather it is a perceptive analysis of society, stressing the need for a government of morality as opposed to absolutism. Constant concedes that warfare and the pursuit of glory might perhaps have been justified in a simpler age; it is the rise of militarism, harnessed to industrialism and government subjugation of the press, that raises the specter of self-perpetuating wars of conquest. With profound insight, Constant foresaw the rise of the totalitarian state and the cynical distortion of revolutionary ideals by oligarchies that control all public means of expression. It is a timeless work that establishes Constant as an impressive political thinker and helps rectify the picture of a weak-willed libertine.

Unfortunately, the positive effect of this eloquent denunciation of Napoleon was largely negated by Constant's attempt to make Bernadotte ruler of the French. Like Mme de Staël, he had been out of the country too long and had lost touch with the prevailing mood; though the nation was tired of war, there was little enthusiasm to accept a man who had fought against his homeland. When Benjamin reached Paris on April 15, 1814, in the wake of the allied armies, he realized that his gamble to place Bernadotte on the throne had failed. A lifelong critic of despotic rule, he had carelessly thrown away his best cards for political advancement in one play.

On May 13 Benjamin went to visit Germaine, newly arrived in Paris from London. Ravaged by the cumulative effects of opium, spiritless and haggard, she remained indifferent to Benjamin's lack of official recognition, even chiding him for not sympathizing sufficiently with France's plight: "You are not French, Benjamin," was her summation of his shortcomings. With no political prospects in view, he indulged in one last outrageous folly: he fell head over heels in love with Juliette Récamier. He should have known better, having witnessed countless suitors over the years court this unyielding beauty in vain. Incredibly, he wrote impassioned letters to both Juliette and Charlotte, who had remained in Germany, meanwhile publishing political essays that gave the appearance of defending contradictory positions. Benjamin saw it otherwise; his principles remained firm while events and personalities were constantly changing.

The Hundred Days gave Constant an opportunity to prove his political acumen, or, according to his detractors, his chameleon-like ability to ingratiate himself with whatever régime happened to be in power. Up to the very moment of the ex-Emperor's return to Paris, Constant had attacked him bitterly, comparing him to Attila and Genghis Khan. Still under the sway of the coy Juliette —as were Auguste de Staël and the Duke of Wellington, to name but two of her more prominent victims—Benjamin sought to impress her with his anti-Napoleonic fervor. Accordingly, in the *Journal des Débats,* he declared that he was prepared to die in defense of the Bourbons; the following day Napoleon entered Paris, and Benjamin, regarding America as a possible refuge, fled first to the American legation and then to Angers on the road to Nantes. The next moves are *déjà vu;* Benjamin did not lay down his life for anyone, least of all for Louis XVIII, and stealing back to Paris undetected, approached Fouché and the incredibly forbearing Joseph, hoping they would put in a good word with the restored Emperor.

In his *Memoirs of the Hundred Days,* Constant defends his decision to assist Napoleon:

> I have been slanderously accused of not having killed myself for the throne I had defended on the 19th of March; but on the 20th I raised my eyes, and I saw that the throne had disappeared and that France still remained. . . . I thought that if Bonaparte were acting in good faith in his offer to submit himself to liberty, he deserved to be supported, and that if he were not acting in good faith, advantage should be taken to turn his own stratagem against him and break in his hands the instrument he wished to set aside.

This was a reference to a new Assembly that would also contain vigorous opponents to any reimposition of dictatorial policies. Constant's position was not only valid but consistent with his political thought; it was the effusive article praising the Bourbons that was out of keeping with his beliefs. Benjamin's later defense was clear in that his advocacy of individual liberty and representative government never wavered, whereas the régimes of those uncertain times had proven unstable and without real convictions.

With Napoleon back in the Tuileries as a fact of life, Constant took stock of the situation. He had supported the King until the last moment because at least he had been surrounded by Frenchmen; now there loomed the threat of a foreign invasion threatening national independence. The vital need, as Constant saw it, was the creation of a responsible government which would forestall a renewal of the imperial dictatorship. After thirteen years in opposition, it would not be easy to work with Napoleon, but already in the Council of State the speeches were outspoken and courageous. Even more remarkable was Napoleon's acceptance of the new tone, so that Constant was neither surprised nor apprehensive when he received an invitation to the Tuileries. His interview with Napoleon was entirely without rancor or recrimination on either side. Each understood and respected the other's position, but Constant knew that Napoleon had not changed inwardly:

> I did not believe at all, as I have already said, in the sudden conversion of a man who for so long has exercised the most absolute authority; the habits of despotism are hardly ever lost. At the same time, I did not fear any persecution; it had been shown to me that Bonaparte's enemies for the moment had nothing to fear. He was sounding out opinion, giving everyone time to escape; he would only have become terrible again the moment he made up his mind to establish a dictatorship. I felt myself perfectly free; I could refuse any cooperation which I foresaw would be proposed to me. It depended on me whether to go at all to the Tuileries, to live alone, or to leave France and to await the future in peace; it was my choice that I accepted the invitation that was addressed to me.

Constant was rallying to Napoleon when the latter was at his weakest and had only unknown perils to offer; yet this man, who had been recognized by every monarch in Europe for over a decade, was now the only person who could bring stability to France, that is, if he could be persuaded to accept effective constitutional government. To Constant, Napoleon grudgingly admitted the need at that moment for parliamentary institutions:

> The nation has rested for twelve years from any political agitation, and for one year from war. This double rest has given it a need for activity. It wants, or thinks it wants, a Tribunate and Assemblies. It did not always want them. It threw itself at my feet when I took over the government. You must recall that, you who tried to form an Opposition. Where was your support, your strength? Nowhere. I took upon myself less authority than I was invited to assume.... Today, everything has changed.

Napoleon protested that only a minority of the nation wanted a Constitution, debates, and so forth. What they really wanted was his return, which was not a military conquest but a popular movement. He himself came from the people, which explained the bond between them: "They regard me as their support, their savior against the nobles.... I just have to make a sign, or rather avert my gaze, and the nobles will be massacred in all the provinces." For one who had a secret liking for the trappings of the aristocracy this is a strange utterance, tending to bear out Metternich's assertion that Napoleon brought back the Revolution from Elba.

Switching his ground, Napoleon assured Constant that he was now content to limit himself to ruling France and not the world, and that he no longer regarded himself as a conqueror. He was vigorously in favor of a free press, open elections, public discussions, and working with responsible ministers; he foresaw a difficult struggle against his enemies who were determined to inflict a war against him, even though his sole wish was to be a constitutional monarch. Constant comprehended that Napoleon had decided to portray the moderate, the conciliator who would rally as many divergent elements around him as possible.

Some Magna Carta was required, and who was better suited than Benjamin Constant to prepare such a document?

The *Acte additionnel aux Constitutions de l'Empire*, the full title of Constant's necessarily hasty work, was unfortunately named, for its author intended it to be forward-looking, a hope for the future rather than an extension of the past. On this point he remonstrated in vain with Napoleon, who insisted on some link with the Empire:

> You are depriving me of my past; I want to keep it. What are you doing to my eleven years of rule? I have some rights to that, I think, and Europe knows it. The new Constitution must be attached to the old. It will have the sanction of glory and success.

Constant protested that it would require more popularity than mere past memories, but finally gave in. At least he had gained a true National Assembly with safeguards against arbitrary power; following the English pattern, it was to be given an independent role, thus protecting it from intrusion on the part of the executive. Constant was well aware of the Constitution's shortcomings, e.g., its silence on the question of confiscation of property, which Napoleon argued was a necessary weapon against the nation's enemies. While conceding that *La Benjamine*— as Constant's work was derisively referred to by the populace—contained many imperfections, at least it represented a substantial advance, such as trial by jury (in civil cases) rather than by military tribunal as had often been the practice. Chateaubriand told Louis XVIII at Ghent that the *Acte additionnel* was an improvement on the proposed Bourbon Charter:

> Bonaparte's new Constitution is a homage to your wisdom; it is with few differences the Constitutional Charter. Bonaparte has only anticipated, with his usual

rudeness, the improvements and completions that you were wisely contemplating.... Napoleon has entangled himself in his own documents; the *Acte additionnel* will be fatal to him; if this document is carried out, there is enough liberty in it to overthrow the tyrant.

Had the *Acte additionnel* been composed in a calmer period, it would have been discussed article by article in the Assembly, and many of the weaknesses eliminated. Constant felt that the laws were only as effective as the Assembly itself, and events were to prove him right. Having acted from purely patriotic motives, he found that his work had alienated republicans and royalists, Bonapartists, and even liberals, each group bitterly resenting some omission or concession: "Never was blame more bitter, never was condemnation more unanimous." Napoleon taxed Constant with its failure: "Well, the new Constitution is not going to succeed," to which its author retorted: "People don't believe in it, make them believe by carrying it out." In later years Constant was proud to contend that freedom was greater and punishment less during the Hundred Days than under the royalist restoration. One day Fouché had confided to him: "Violent measures, far from overcoming resistance, just give birth to new by giving it more strength. Continue your work, don't get discouraged; come and talk to me." A visiting Englishman declared that he found more liberty in France during this brief period than in his own country; to the anglophile Benjamin, there was no greater compliment.

The defeat at Waterloo dashed the hopes of the newly appointed Counselor of State who had enjoyed the resplendent uniform and remuneration for a few short weeks. There followed two lengthy conversations with the defeated Emperor on his return to Paris. The first meeting took place at the Elysée Palace and lasted three hours; Napoleon was "serious, but calm." He still had a sizable army at his disposal with which he could forcibly disband the Assembly that was now calling for his abdication. At that moment, his musings were interrupted by the shouts of *"Vive l'Empereur!"* from a crowd gathering in the street outside. "You see," he said, "these are not those whom I heaped with honors and wealth. What do they owe me? I found them poor and I have left them poor. It is the instinct of necessity that lights their path, the voice of the country speaks through them; if I want to, if I allow it, then within one hour the rebel Assembly will exist no more.... But the life of one man is not worth such a price. I did not come back from the isle of Elba to drown Paris in blood." Benjamin was greatly moved by Napoleon's consideration, adding a generous sentiment of his own: "He who ... divests himself of power rather than disputes it by massacres and civil war, on that occasion has deserved well of the human race." The two men met once more on June 24 to discuss their respective situations, bade one another a warm farewell, then departed to their separate destinies.

Years later, a short time before his own death, Constant looked back upon this amazing man:

> Bonaparte was a man of immense genius; he was better suited than any other to dominate an enthusiastic nation in a period of military glory, a people that occasionally forgot the pleasures of liberty due to the fame and pride of victory. But Bonaparte, son of the Republic, had plotted his own ruin. To bring it about, he had to work ceaselessly at the destruction not only of the republican forms to which the nation was not attached, but also of the principles which the nation had proclaimed in 1789 and wished to see applied, working amid crimes of terror, ineptitude, under a Directory sometimes fainthearted, sometimes vindictive, and amid the dazzling pomp of imperial conquests.... The world has been punished for having corrupted him; he has been punished for allowing himself to be corrupted.

In retrospect, Constant believed that the attempt at constitutional government in 1815 was a mistake without popular support, but he insisted that extraordinary conditions—*la patrie en danger*—had called for extraordinary measures. To the end he regarded himself as a patriot who had selflessly acted in his country's best interests.

Napoleon's overthrow placed Benjamin in great danger. Fortunately, Louis XVIII personally was not vindictive and even admired his opponent's dexterity, sensing, perhaps, that they had much in common. Benjamin, realizing the futility of pursuing either a parliamentary career or the coquettish Juliette, decided to spend several months in England with Charlotte, who had awaited him with her customary patience. For some years he had been gaining a literary reputation in social circles by declaiming *Adolphe* before sentimental audiences; the steady flow of tears could not be transmuted into steady income, and so he decided in 1816 to have the novel published simultaneously in London and Paris. As Charlotte could not withstand the English climate—one of history's constants—they cut their stay short and returned to Paris.

Though Benjamin still occasionally corresponded with Mme de Staël, she showed little desire to renew the old acquaintanceship. Only on her deathbed in 1817 did he gaze again upon the woman who had deprived him of his middle years. During her last illness she had discouraged his visits, and she was already dead when he was admitted into her presence for the last time. Only now could he have felt truly free to live as husband and wife with Charlotte; for both of them, a new life was beginning at the age of fifty.

After the Bourbon restoration and until his death in 1830, he was the acknowledged liberal spokesman in the Chamber, often demonstrating great resolution in stemming the reactionary tide. He became an eloquent proponent of the complete freedom of the individual vis-à-vis government encroachment, an unyielding advocate of democracy based on the voluntary acceptance of the law. Both by nature and political philosophy he was incapable of leading a parliamentary party; to the very end he was regarded with both admiration and suspicion, praised for his intellect but also distrusted for past vacillations. He saw his role as that of the gadfly and enlightener, the conscience of democracy.

Many questions remain unanswered. Did Mme de Staël help or destroy the young man who stopped her carriage in 1794? Did she merely precipitate an inevitable clash with Bonaparte or might Constant have counteracted the latter's political excesses much as Fouché and Talleyrand, each in his way, strove to do? Or was Benjamin, "constant in his opinions despite the inconstancy of his heart" (Pozzo di Borgo's telling aphorism), incapable of compromising with a dictator on the ascent? Twice he placed his talents at the service of Napoleon and twice he failed; yet if one is prepared to overlook his preposterous private life, one can discern a mind of great nobility. Had the cards willed otherwise, Napoleon and Benjamin might have saved one another.

Joseph Fouché

The story is told that once, in a fit of exasperation, Napoleon bitterly complained to his brother Louis about his ubiquitous Minister of Police: "One day he's prying into my bed and the next day into my private papers." On both accounts the accusation rang true; Joseph Fouché, Duke of Otranto, Minister of Police, knew as much about Napoleon's affairs, both financial and amatory, as the Emperor himself. On one occasion Napoleon unwisely reprimanded Fouché for his supposed lack of vigilance, whereupon the police commissioner gave a detailed description of the nocturnal visits of a stout gentleman to the famous Italian opera singer, the beautiful Grassini: "This little man is yourself to whom the whimsical singer is unfaithful to the advantage of Rode, the violinist." Fouché not only survived to relate the anecdote but was later reappointed to the same vital post during the Hundred

Days. Despised and feared during his lifetime, he made it his business to be indispensable to whatever government happened to be in power. "He is certainly the most cunning of the lot" was Napoleon's summation before appointing Fouché as Minister of Police for the third time. Notwithstanding the formidable devious talents of Talleyrand, Fouché's great rival, posterity has seen little reason to quarrel with Napoleon's encomium.

Like so many men who wield effective power during a time of profound change, Fouché preferred to work in the shadows rather than in the glare of day. A meticulous mole unearthing a mountain of information brought to him by a vast network of spies, he rejected the outward signs of authority for the more durable reality. Whereas his contemporaries strove to garner the honors and glory of the Consulate and Empire, Fouché was solely interested in acquiring detailed knowledge that might enable him to play a dominant role in the affairs of state. True, he was by no means indifferent to titles and wealth, but these were incidental to the satisfaction derived from controlling the lives of millions. His justification for his actions was simple: "Every government requires as a chief guarantee of its safety a vigilant police, with firm and clear-sighted chiefs," he wrote in his *Memoirs* which—typical of the man—he may well not have written at all. (Heine, in a cynical comment, observed that Fouché "carried his falseness to such lengths as to publish false memoirs after his death"—a feat amazing even by Fouché's standards). A more accurate observation is Talleyrand's barbed quip that the "Minister of Police is a man who minds his own business—and goes on to mind other people's." But we are *in medias res*—the beginnings are far more modest.

Joseph Fouché was born near the Atlantic port of Nantes either in 1759 or 1760. It soon became clear that the frail youth would be ill-suited to a life at sea, so he was entrusted to the care of the Oratorians, a religious order primarily engaged in teaching. At the school in Paris, young Joseph learned the virtues of mental discipline and self-control, eschewing all excesses or vices. These characteristics predominated throughout his life, to which must be added an innate wariness and suspicion. Thus, Fouché never took his final vows, even though he remained with the Oratorians as a teacher of science and mathematics in Arras. Here he became acquainted with the future general Carnot and a rising lawyer named Maximilien Robespierre, to whom he lent sufficient money for the journey to Paris, having briefly courted the latter's sister. The romance came to nothing, and shortly after the outbreak of the Revolution, Fouché returned to his hometown.

The Oratorians were sympathetic to reform, and in February 1791, Fouché became president of the local *Les Amis de la Constitution*. Nantes was mildly royalist in its outlook, and though Fouché was an ineffective orator, his diligence and moderation impressed his fellow citizens sufficiently to elect him to the National Convention in Paris. It was here that he met his future wife, Bonne-Jeanne Coiquand, an ungainly woman to whom he remained touchingly attached and faithful for life.

As an uncommitted liberal, Fouché tended to ally himself with the more moderate Girondists, working effectively behind the scenes on committees and special commissions. Such anonymity could not last indefinitely during a period of rising fanaticism, and Robespierre's insistence on a public vote to decide the fate of Louis XVI made further evasion impossible. Fouché, though personally in favor of sparing the King's life, had correctly assessed the upsurge in radical fervor and voted for *la mort*. This unprincipled change of mind was sufficient to produce the single vote majority required; henceforth, until his death, Fouché was branded as a regicide.

Having escaped the fate of the Girondists, Fouché nevertheless was uncomfortably aware that his ex-friend Robespierre viewed his vacillations with great distrust. When the National Convention sent him to his native Nantes to organize the militia against the royalist rising in the Vendée, Fouché welcomed the opportunity to escape the Terror. By now the Oratorian teacher had become an impassioned atheist, indeed, even a revolutionary socialist. Both in Nevers and in Troyes he confiscated private property and pillaged churches for gold and silver with which to bolster government finances in Paris and to impress those in power. On his own initiative he urged priests to marry or adopt children, at the same time denying the existence of a life hereafter by declaring officially that "death is an eternal sleep." Such revolutionary zeal deserved a reward, and when Lyon (as did many provincial cities) rejected the authority of the government in Paris, a stern hand was called for. Following the capitulation of the city—now renamed Ville Affranchie—Fouché and an ex-actor named Collot d'Herbois were sent by the Convention to destroy the city as an object lesson and to execute all citizens who had taken part in the uprising. Understandably enough, there is no mention of the ensuing destruction and slaughter in the *Memoirs*; in a matter of a few weeks over 1600 victims were mowed down by the *mitraillade,* a cannon filled with grapeshot, and then thrown into a common grave or tossed into the Rhone.

On February 6, 1794, Fouché ordered the end of the mass shootings, though the guillotine continued on a more selective basis. The ex-Oratorian had come to realize that the senseless shootings were defeating any purpose they might originally have had by creating an atmosphere of vicious denunciations in which guilty and innocent alike perished. This lesson had a profound effect on his later career: it was more effective from every standpoint merely to execute a leader or two and then allow their followers to ruminate on their fate. Significantly, the last two executions ordered by Fouché in Lyon were those of the executioner and his assistant. The Convention was not impressed and demanded that Fouché return to Paris to account for his "moderation." A more serious charge was his unbridled atheism; Robespierre, now filled with moral rectitude, had declared the doctrine of the Supreme Being, implying his own infallibility, and called upon Fouché to explain himself before the dreaded Committee of Public Safety, a summons tantamount to a sentence of death.

Fouché now found himself in a desperate situation. As a representative of the Convention he requested that he make his report to that body rather than before Robespierre's chosen instrument. Never spending more than a night or two under the same roof in order to avoid arrest, Fouché undermined his dangerous rival by uniting and instilling courage in the latter's prospective victims, and was even elected president of the radical Jacobin Club, much to Robespierre's vexation. Indeed, many of the Incorruptible's followers had become increasingly critical of his arrogance and despotism, and the empty seats in the Convention made up for any eloquence that Fouché lacked. Robespierre's end was swift and sure; having failed to convince the representatives of the validity of his accusations, the tyrant was later shouted down in the Convention, arrested, and executed. Though the Terror had ended, Fouché as an ex-terrorist himself still ran the danger of the "dry guillotine"—near certain death in the penal colonies of Guiana. Only by blaming others, including his colleague Collot, and by denying all responsibility did he manage to escape their fate. Fouché had lost everything: his position, fortune and fame, all, except his life and his faithful Bonne-Jeanne.

Very little is known about Fouché's movements in the years between 1794 and 1797. Reduced to living in a miserable garret, he seems to have been involved in dubious banking transactions and smuggling before acting as a spy for Barras, one of the five Directors who now ruled France. At first working in the provinces, Fouché returned to Paris to help Barras put an end to the Babeuf conspiracy, which sought to retain the purity of the Revolution, and later prepare a coup d'état aimed at his fellow Directors. A grateful Barras was anxious to reward his protégé, but Fouché himself tells us: "However, I persisted in refusing the subordinate favors offered me; I was resolved to accept a brilliant mission only, one that would start me suddenly in the career of great political affairs. I had the patience to wait; I even waited a long time, but I did not wait in vain." Eventually he was appointed Ambassador to the Cisalpine Republic (formed by Bonaparte in northern Italy in 1797) and later to Holland, where in both posts his enlightened and liberal policies were successful. Barras was impressed, and mindful of his own precarious position at home, recalled Fouché to Paris to appoint him Minister of Police.

The department that he inherited was riddled with corruption and inefficiency in a society engaged in speculation and high living. Fouché soon centralized the control of the department, and to finance a growing network of spies he levied a tax on gambling and prostitution, infallible sources of revenue: "The treasury was empty; and without money, no police is possible. I soon had money in my treasury by making vice, inherent to all great cities, tributary to the police of the State." To give himself a freer hand and to escape public criticism, he suppressed many of the newspapers and personally closed the doors of the Jacobin Club to which he owed so much. Though he kept an observant eye on royalist activities, Fouché also allowed many of the minor émigrés to return on the theory that conciliation, besides proving an effective policy, would also place many a grateful person in his debt. He was able to justify his extensive spy system and copious dossiers on thousands of citizens by pointing out that France enjoyed greater stability at home than ever before. With the advent of 18 Brumaire and Napoleon's rise to power, Fouché transformed boast into reality.

As Minister of Police he was naturally aware that yet another coup, this time directed by Bonaparte against the conniving Barras and the Directory, was under way. Barras had appointed Fouché precisely for the purpose of forestalling such a conspiracy; unfortunately, he failed to recognize that Fouché's loyalties were devoted to the party with the best prospects. Through Josephine, whom he had liberally bribed, Fouché knew about Napoleon's early return from Egypt and his future plans, and was therefore able to act accordingly. When the conspirators struck, Barras was somehow caught by Mme Tallien in his bath—an embarrassing situation, so to speak—while the coup itself was under way at St. Cloud, some distance from the capital. Fouché had tricked the two legislative councils into meeting here for their own protection, and for added security had the entrances to Paris sealed off by special detachments. Just in case the coup should fail (as it very nearly did due to Bonaparte's uninspired performance) Fouché had arranged for a relay of messengers to report to him at half-hour intervals on the progress of events. The Minister of Police was thus in a position either to hail the success of the coup or else suppress it vigorously should it fail. No doubt he had learned from the gambling fraternity that all horses in the race should be covered.

Thus began a bizarre alliance that was only to end with Napoleon's political demise fifteen years later. On the one hand, the self-proclaimed genius given to temperamental outbursts and passionate action; on the other, the unemotional police official, relentlessly gathering information on everyone and everything, discreet but just as anxious to exercise power as his master. Without Fouché's efficiency and constant awareness of all that was happening in France, it is doubtful whether Napoleon could have absented himself for such protracted periods to wage his foreign wars. In a very real sense, Fouché's presence— no matter how inimical their personal relationship might have been—was a vital element in the conduct of Napoleon's policies both at home and abroad.

Had the First Consul and later Emperor relied solely on his Minister of Police for confidential information, it is probable that many of the subsequent mistakes would have been avoided. As it was, Fouché had to compete with Napoleon's own spies and those of Talleyrand and Lucien Bonaparte, as well as those of the military and other ministries. Many spies and informers worked for more than one master, and many an official earned a supplementary income by passing on information. Fouché later admitted that he had paid Duroc, Napoleon's secretary, 25,000 francs a month to spy on his master; for good measure Louis XVIII's cook in England was also in the pay of the Minister of Police. This vast network of competing spy systems resulted in the four separate reports that Napoleon received each day, often mutually contradictory and inaccurate.

Nor did the press and theatre fare any better. The *Moniteur* frequently carried planted articles, distorted news, and Napoleon's exaggerated accounts of his campaigns. Plays and novels were censored as a matter of course, and not even the opera was totally immune from manipulation. During a performance of *The Horatii* a sham attack on Bonaparte, in the audience, was arranged by Fouché, who candidly confessed later, "every government at its dawn usually takes advantage of a danger it has created, either to make it more firm, or to extend its power; all it needs is to escape a conspiracy to acquire more strength and influence."

Fouché found himself faced with two difficult crises in his first year as Bonaparte's Minister of Police. Having assured himself that all was well at home, the First Consul in his capacity as military leader set off across the Great St. Bernard pass to fall on the Austrians who had reoccupied northern Italy. News of a decisive battle was awaited hourly in Paris. The first reports indicated that the French had suffered a defeat, which in turn would have meant the end of Bonaparte's further political ambitions. Fouché vacillated, unsure which way to jump; only when it became apparent that Marengo had indeed been a brilliant victory did he resume full control. Bonaparte hereafter regarded his minister with distrust; as Fouché himself admitted, at Marengo the First Consul had conquered France and would henceforth be the undisputed ruler.

The second crisis involved a genuine assassination attempt on Christmas Eve, 1800, as Napoleon and Josephine were driving in their carriages to a performance of Haydn's *Creation*. Although rumors had abounded the previous day, the First Consul's own police (but not Fouché's) had assured him that both the route and the theatre had been inspected and nothing of a suspicious nature found. Just after Bonapare turned into the narrow Rue St. Nicaise a *machine infernale*—a cart filled with gunpowder—exploded; but miraculously its intended victim escaped without injury, as the driver of the First Consul's carriage drove faster than usual due to inebriation—an inspired case of drunken driving. Fouché was given a tongue-lashing and insulted to his face; he should have kept an eye on his Jacobin friends who were responsible for the outrage. Fouché calmly offered to prove within two weeks that the plot was the work of the royalists. Literally piecing the evidence together, a blacksmith was found who recognized a horseshoe from one of the dead animals as being his work. The trail led to the arrest of the royalist conspirators, who confessed all before they were executed. Bonaparte was impressed by the efficiency of his chief of police, but nevertheless could not forego the opportunity to deport several innocent Jacobins to Africa.

Though disagreeing on many issues, Bonaparte and Fouché were both aware that the mass of the people were tired of corruption and inflation, as well as rhetorical calls for liberty. What the nation sought was order and even some of the social graces of the *ancien régime*. Thus, the early months of the Consulate were marked by moderation and enlightened government, which in turn produced a national sense of stability and purpose. Bonaparte, moving towards the political right, declared a general amnesty to the vast majority of émigrés, though pointedly excluding Louis XVIII. On March 25, 1802, the treaty of Amiens was signed between England and France amid outbursts of popular enthusiasm from a nation weary of ten years of revolutionary wars. These policies also reflected the convictions of Fouché, who believed that France could now embark on programs of social and economic development. On Easter Sunday the bells of Notre Dame rang for the first time in many years to celebrate peace with a *Te Deum* at which the First Consul, apparently having become a good Catholic, was present.

Together with many of the republican generals and politicians, Fouché had opposed the ratification of the previous year's Concordat with Rome, regarding it as a cynical act to unify the people for political reasons. The Peace of Amiens and the Concordat were twin preludes to Bonaparte's having himself elected Consul for life, the first step towards becoming Emperor. The new Caesar expressed his thanks by reducing the Senate and Tribunate to mere ciphers; men of genius must not be impeded by those of lesser vision. Fouché turned to his master in vain: "Truly, I saw in all this only a shapeless and dangerous work; and I expressed myself to that effect without concealment. I told the First Consul that he had just declared himself the head of a life monarchy which, in my opinion, had no other foundation than his sword and his victories." By now Bonaparte had become jealous of Fouché's growing reputation. For the first time he became receptive to criticism of his Minister of Police from his numerous brothers and sisters who, if in nothing else, were united in their hostility towards Fouché and Josephine. In August 1802, Fouché was informed by the Head of State that he had performed his duties so well that his post was no longer necessary. In recognition of his services he was to be given over a million francs and be made a senator to show that there were no ill feelings in the matter. The First Consul was taking no risks; men of Fouché's ability might be required in the future.

By May 1803 Europe was again at war. Fouché in less than ten years had progressed from living in a garret to owning sumptuous houses in the Rue Cerutti, in Ferrières near Paris, and in Aix in the southern part of the country; nevertheless, his relative inactivity made him restless and anxious to regain his former position. The opportunity came when a group of royalist conspirators entered Paris undetected by the police. The plot—which implicated two of France's most renowned generals—was discovered only at the last moment. Bonaparte, influenced by his Corsican upbringing and inaccurate information, swore revenge and ordered the secret arrest in Germany of the duc d'Enghien, whom he presumed to be the royal prince behind the intrigue. The innocent victim of Bonaparte's wrath was taken to a fortress near Paris, tried by the First Consul's brother-in-law, and shot, all within a matter of a few hours. Fouché had interceded to no avail, pointing out the dire political effects of such an ill-considered act and affront to legality. "This is worse than a crime, it's a blunder" was his famous summation. The blunder was to unite France's enemies and plunge Europe into eleven years of warfare. On July 10, 1804, Fouché was recalled as Minister of Police.

The Enghien affair marked a definite breach between Bonaparte and the Bourbons. Though at heart still a republican, Fouché realized that national stability took precedence over personal feelings. Accordingly, in the Senate he encouraged the creation of the Empire, which was established on May 18, 1804. The relationship between master and servant became increasingly formal, so that Fouché hesitated to speak to the Emperor with his former frankness (needless to say, Napoleon felt no such inhibitions and continued to insult his minister to his face and behind his back). This in no way prevented Fouché from keeping the imperial boudoir under surveillance; indeed, Fouché was one of the first to suspect that it was Josephine (in spite of her two children by her first marriage) and not Napoleon who was unable to produce an heir. The Emperor's private police had few such piquant domestic details to report to their master, as Fouché neither smoked, drank to excess, nor was he ever unfaithful to his wife—in brief, a paragon of supposed Napoleonic virtues. At the very most he might have been cited for un-French activities.

During the Emperor's frequent foreign campaigns Fouché became the effective ruler of France. His method was to persuade rather than punish, and this was possible only through an extensive spy system. Fouché's proud boast was that "where three are met together, I have always one listening," an exaggeration that well suited his purposes by discouraging conspiracies. Even his enemies grudgingly conceded his moderation and enlightened policies. Madame de Staël, one of Napoleon's most consistent opponents, admitted that the Minister of Police "did no more wrong than necessity required," and though frequently banished from Paris, on occasion she managed to slip into the capital while Fouché looked the other way. For this act of calculated negligence Fouché was reprimanded in unequivocal terms by Napoleon, who had been informed in distant Poland by his own spies. To balance matters, Fouché received daily reports on the progress of the Emperor's affair with the Countess Marie Walewska.

Having suppressed the majority of newspapers at home and censored the remaining ones, Fouché could devote much of his time to culling material from foreign gazettes, which formed an essential part of his daily reports to Napoleon. Foreign diplomats were spied upon as a matter of course, and the issuing or withholding of passports for travel lay entirely within Fouché's province. He was well aware that it was becoming increasingly difficult to separate domestic from expansionist policies abroad and that the latter, if left unchecked, would bring about the ultimate ruin of the Empire. It was clear that Napoleon's armies were draining the country of its youth and prosperity, while his ambitions became more grandiose with each new campaign.

The attack on Spain in 1808 and the news of the first reverses suffered on the battlefield brought about a political union that astounded Parisian society. For years, Talleyrand, the Foreign Minister, and Fouché—despite their similar ecclesiastical background—had not been on speaking terms, a situation that delighted Napoleon. A common desire for peace motivated them to stage a public reconciliation and to lay plans for the future. Napoleon, sensing a revolt, hurriedly returned from Spain and dismissed Talleyrand in a highly emotional scene; Fouché, as usual, rode out the storm. The following year, the Emperor's absence in Austria gave rise to a far more critical situation. The English landing at Walcheren in the Netherlands was a direct threat to Antwerp and northern France, and needed to be repulsed at once. On his own initiative, Fouché mobilized the National Guard and appointed General Bernadotte, already out of favor with the Emperor, as its commander. In a patriotic letter Fouché declared: "Let us prove to Europe that if the genius of Napoleon can add lustre to France, his presence is not necessary to drive back the enemy," a statement lacking in tact but, as the successful counterattack proved, completely accurate. The Emperor was obliged to conceal his rage, and a week later Fouché was elevated to the title of Duke of Otranto.

Unaccountably, Fouché now committed a series of mistakes that led to his second dismissal. Perhaps grown overconfident, he again called up the National Guard, this time unfortunately for a nonexistent invasion. This was followed by an act of political opportunism and betrayal. Fouché now turned on Josephine and impudently advised her to facilitate a divorce, for which he was roundly scolded by Napoleon, who lacked the courage to make a similar suggestion. A far more serious error in judgment arose when Fouché decided to play the statesman and secure peace with England, not only without the Emperor's knowledge but also by using his name in the secret negotiations. For once, Fouché neglected to take sufficient precautions and was taken completely by surprise when a furious Napoleon confronted him with his duplicity. On July 3, 1810, Fouché was dismissed, and Savary, an insensitive army general, was appointed Minister of Police.

Fouché's downfall was regretted by many who had benefited from his considerate treatment. Aware of his minister's wide popularity, Napoleon appointed him Governor of Rome, but before he could leave to take up the post, the Emperor was informed by Savary that his predecessor had burned several secret files. The indignant Emperor demanded that the remaining private correspondence and other vital material be returned at once; Fouché complied in part to gain time before fleeing to Italy. Eventually he was allowed to return to France, only to suffer the tragic loss of his wife, who died in 1812. Though now an extremely wealthy man, Fouché was faced with an empty life unless events came to his aid. In late October of the same year, at the time of Napoleon's disastrous retreat from Moscow, such an event occurred in Paris.

Under Savary's command of the police, it soon became apparent that severity was a poor substitute for surveillance. Accordingly, when General Malet, a persistent conspirator against Napoleon, escaped from prison, Savary was unaware of his movements or intentions. Malet's plan, in fact, was simplicity itself; he declared that Napoleon had died in Russia and that a provisional government had taken over. Though Malet had Savary placed under arrest, he failed to act decisively and the coup d'état collapsed. Napoleon was thoroughly alarmed that a plot could so nearly succeed and find such widespread support on the basis of a mere rumor. Worse still, Savary's police had failed to crush the conspiracy in its early stages; such inefficiency could not be tolerated. Fouché was delighted at Savary's discomfiture, and gained further satisfaction when Napoleon summoned him to Dresden to seek his advice, the closest the Emperor ever came to admitting that he had been mistaken.

Fouché was now approaching his mid-fifties, and though as slender and angular as ever, his waning energies seemed to match the declining fortunes of the Empire. In uncharacteristic fashion, he wasted four months trying to influence the various factions in Italy before he returned to Paris too late—Louis XVIII was already on the throne with Talleyrand in command. Fouché wisely declined a government post, having already dismissed the Bourbons with the comment that "we shan't have them for more than a year." Though personally in favor of peace and opposed to Napoleon's return, the myopic attitude of many of the returned émigrés convinced him that the royalist régime would be of brief duration; the news of the Emperor's landing and triumphant advance came as no surprise. At the last moment the Bourbons decided to arrest Fouché, who in the best tradition of the French bedroom farce managed to escape over a wall with the help of a ladder, landing in the back garden of Hortense, Napoleon's stepdaughter and, incidentally, sister-in-law. Upon the ex-Emperor's arrival, Fouché was immediately renamed Minister of Police.

Of all the ministers who served during the Hundred Days, Fouché was by far the most capable and was widely regarded as the only effective bridge between Napoleon and the royalists. As such, he entered into secret negotiations with Metternich behind the Emperor's back, but on this occasion he was well-prepared when Napoleon shouted at him: "You are a traitor! I ought to have you hanged!" "Sire," he replied, "I do not share Your Majesty's opinion." Fouché revealed his discovery that Napoleon had laid a trap for him at the *Drei Könige* Hotel in Basle where the diplomatic meeting with Metternich's representative was to take place; the Emperor shouted for an hour but finally had to acknowledge himself beaten. This skirmish was but a minor prelude to the decisive defeat suffered at Waterloo. Fouché saw the imperative need for Napoleon to abdicate, and as the temporary head of government he was in a position to force the ex-Emperor to leave Paris and make way once again for Louis XVIII.

Despite the King's dislike of one who had voted for his brother's death, Fouché was appointed Minister of Police for the fourth time. Louis XVIII is supposed to have uttered: "Unfortunate brother! If you saw me, you would pardon me." Though the King later honored Fouché by attending his wedding to a beautiful girl some thirty years younger than himself, it was clear that the Minister of Police had outlived his usefulness once the Bourbons had reestablished themselves. The Duchess d'Angoulême, the strong-willed daughter of Louis XVI and Marie Antoinette—"the only man in the family" according to Napoleon—bitterly disliked the regicidal minister, and prevailed upon her uncle to dismiss him and send him into virtual exile.

The last five years of Fouché's life were spent wandering between Prague, Munich, and Linz, at each move having to beg a haughty Metternich for asylum. The former police commissioner had no need for any spies to discover whether his young wife was engaged in *une amitié amoureuse* with another man; the answer was written in the eyes and lips of those with whom he still came in contact. Finally he found solace in Trieste, where Jerome and Elisa Bonaparte showed him great kindness, no doubt in part for some of the discreet services Fouché had rendered them in the past. The end came on December 20, 1820; the ex-Oratorian, terrorist, Jacobin, atheist, and part-time royalist finally made his peace with the Church and was buried in hallowed ground.

To find the focal point in such an opportunistic career is indeed difficult. If, by a convenient lapse of memory, one can overlook Fouché's terrible beginnings in Lyon and the Convention, his later actions take on a definite consistency. Essentially they were those of an enlightened democrat of the eighteenth century who believed in an ordered society which would ensure the welfare of the citizenry. Any real progress was predicated on peace and intelligent government, and it was toward the establishment of this twin aim, with, of course, himself in a position of power, that he dedicated his energies. Thus, to Fouché, a police state had none of the terrifying connotations that it has in our own century; perhaps the young student of the classics had learned from the Oratorian fathers that, in Greek, *politeia* meant "the administration of government" in a positive rather than a repressive sense. Had Napoleon listened more attentively to his crafty Minister of Police, he might have avoided becoming the rueful philosopher of St. Helena.

August Wilhelm *Schlegel*

Most Germans are familiar with the name of Schlegel as the inspired translator of Shakespeare, a brilliant achievement that has made the English dramatist in effect Germany's most popular playwright. Students are also aware of Schlegel's pioneering work in romantic literature in collaboration with his wife Caroline and his younger brother Friedrich. No less familiar are his marital troubles and later estrangement from them both, which resulted in his middle years being spent in Coppet as the academic showpiece of Madame de Staël. Schlegel's fame as a critic, linguist, and Sanskrit scholar is well-established and documented; but had he expressed a preference during his own lifetime, he would undoubtedly have wished to be known as a German patriot in the struggle against Napoleon.

Schlegel's interest in politics dated from a very early period of his life. Born in the Hanover of George III in

1767, he was exposed to English culture and ideas as a youth, and acquired the reputation of a Beau Brummell when he went to study at the university in Göttingen. Besides accumulating an impressive amount of learning in classical and modern languages, art, and music, he also participated in heated political discussions on a theoretical level. The main influences on the young student were Schlözer and Heyne, as well as the latter's son-in-law Georg Forster, a radical agitator; a more temperate and lasting friendship was that of Wilhelm von Humboldt, the later diplomat and educator. The profound events of the French Revolution heightened Schlegel's interest in politics, though his basic moderation, even conservatism, is shown in his enthusiastic recommendation of Burke's *Reflections on the Revolution in France* to his brother.

Indeed, Schlegel's elegant appearance, his linguistic gifts, and social contacts indicated that he was destined for a political career. His father wanted him to become secretary to a diplomat in Dresden but the plan fell through, perhaps on account of some trouble he had had with an English student at the university. Whatever the reason, he became instead the private tutor to a family in Amsterdam. This early disappointment portended many of Schlegel's later setbacks; his amazing knowledge in many fields, his wit and courteous charm were in constant conflict with his vanity, pedantry, and lack of personal warmth. Brilliant but lacking in true creativity, learned but unable to conceal his basic prejudices, Schlegel was destined in life to receive qualified praise rather than boundless admiration. Though his writings reveal a mastery of exterior form and a graciousness of expression, they lack force and originality, a reflection of the man himself. Schlegel was keenly aware that his translations from several languages, however brilliant, in the final analysis were the product of the genius who had created the original work. This awareness partly explains his desire to become a politician and thus be a leader rather than a follower.

Schlegel's anti-French attitudes, already pronounced at Göttingen, were reinforced by General Pichegru's occupation of Holland in January 1795 and the proclamation of the Batavian Republic. It is precisely because of his conservative bent that Schlegel was one of the first to recognize the danger of French expansionist policies in the wake of the Revolution. In a letter to a student friend he even defended the status quo of the German principalities by claiming that, whatever their faults, at least they guaranteed the educated segment of the populace "more peace and a happier existence than a regeneration, whereby in the end only cunning and undaunted wickedness prevail." Despite the moderating influence of Caroline, whom he had married in 1796 after considerable hesitation on her part, Schlegel's francophobe feelings remained close to the surface, even though he spoke and wrote the language with the facility of a native.

The following years in Jena and Berlin are well-known to students of German romanticism. But even his famous Berlin lectures on literature and art given in the winters of 1801 to 1803 are not without political overtones. According to Schlegel, only Germany's weakness after the Reformation and foreign intervention during the Thirty Years' War had allowed the French to come to the fore; in fact, their poetry was frivolous, imitative, and of little real value. The political significance of the lectures was not lost on his audience, for the Peace of Lunéville (February 1801) had already resulted in the loss of the left bank of the Rhine; and in May 1803 the fragile peace of the Treaty of Amiens was broken. Schlegel saw that his Hanoverian homeland (then still ruled by the British monarch) was threatened, but his patriotism was confused by an imprecise romantic vision of a resurgent medieval Christian unity. He was proud that Germany had once destroyed a decadent Rome and had risen to imperial greatness under the Hohenstaufen. Various Germanic tribes—the Goths, Franks and Saxons—had helped found other countries and cultures, and Schlegel even claimed that most European languages therefore were of German origin. It was the Reformation that had destroyed this cultural cohesion and divided Germany into warring factions; like many other patriots, Schlegel stressed the spiritual renewal of the nation and the need to look both to the past and the future.

Having stated the problem, Schlegel foresaw the danger lurking between the Scylla of political action and the Charybdis of unwanted revolution. His vision of a rejuvenated Holy Roman Empire had little use for new theories of economics or industrialization which, he predicted, would lead to the oppression of the masses and the creation of a totalitarian state. This attitude, consistent enough in itself, was complicated by Schlegel's francophobia. The Austrian Hapsburgs, he felt, had fallen under French influence to such an extent that they were no longer suited to the role of unifying Germany, and had thus relinquished national leadership to Prussia. This position contrasted sharply with his romantic concept; after all, the modern Prussia being forged by Stein and Scharnhorst had little in common with a vague medievalism. It was only after Prussia's defeat and his brother's acceptance of a diplomatic post in 1809 at the court in Vienna that Schlegel managed to resolve this inner conflict of his own making, and then only until the momentous events of 1813 in which he was to play an active part.

Public acclaim of the Berlin lectures had failed to produce any emotional equilibrium within Schlegel. Respected as a brilliant translator and literary critic, nevertheless he had quarreled with Schiller and had just been divorced from Caroline in May 1803. His friend Novalis had died two years earlier, and an unrequited love for the sister of the German romantic writer, Tieck, hastened the break-up of their literary group. Madame de Staël's arrival in Berlin and her offer of 12,000 francs a year as well as a pension were too much to resist, and so began a ten-year period in Coppet as *un homme de cabinet* away from the German national scene. Schlegel's new duties as tutor and literary adviser certainly did not mean the abandonment of his political interests—under Madame de Staël's aegis, this was a sheer impossibility—but the beginning of a new phase as polemicist rather than as a patriot in arms.

During Bonaparte's first months in power, both Schlegel and Madame de Staël had evidenced an ambivalent attitude towards France's new ruler, even conceiving a romantic admiration which they took no pains to hide. Schlegel's flattering sonnet to the First Consul was received with polite indifference. The subsequent exile of Madame de Staël from France and the French occupation of German territory changed initial regard into personal animosity, so much so that by 1806 Schlegel was calling Napoleon the *"Landerverwüster"* (country devastator). Soon he complained that "all creations of the human spirit within the realm of his might had to wear the livery of bondage." Even visits to Italy and Paris, in spite of the cosmopolitan environment and entrée to a wider society, did little to assuage his negative feelings. Though Madame de Staël had received permission to reside in rural France (but not in the capital), this scant concession was nullified by the news of Prussia's overwhelming defeat at the battle of Jena. Schlegel, whose wide range of cultural interests was the envy of those who knew him, now increasingly narrowed his literary activities to writing patriotic verses. The 1806 campaign against Prussia inspired the following:

> Fremde Sitten, fremde Zungen
> Lernt' ich üben her und hin;
> Nicht im Herzen angeklungen
> Stärkten sie den deutschen Sinn.
> Lang' ein umgetriebner Wandrer,
> Wurd' ich niemals doch ein andrer.
>
> Teure Brüder in Bedrängnis!
> Euch geweiht ist all mein Schmerz.
> Was euch trifft, ist mein Verhängnis;
> Fallt ihr, so begehrt mein Herz,
> Dass nur bald sich mein Gebeine
> Vaterländ'schem Staub vereine.

[I learned to practice foreign customs and languages here and there; but they found no echo in my heart and merely strengthened my German feeling. Though for a long time a driven wanderer, I never changed my allegiance.

Dear, oppressed brothers! I dedicate all my sorrow to you. Whatever assails you is also my fate; if you fall in battle, my heart's only wish is that my bones be soon reunited with the dust of my homeland.]

In Madame de Staël's novel *Corinne,* the hero, Oswald, pauses for a long time before a painting of a scene from *Phèdre*. Schlegel's imagination was aroused; and the result was his *"Comparaison entre la 'Phèdre' de Racine et celle d'Euripide,"* written in French and published in Paris in 1807. This slight work soon became more of a political than a literary *cause célèbre,* interpreted by Napoleon not only as criticism of classical literature but also as an attack upon French culture. The next year Schlegel presented his famous lectures in Vienna on dramatic art and literature, again a theme that seemed innocent enough. However, his audience was receptive to the implied political overtones, for following the Prussian military failures only Austria remained to champion the German cause. Clearly Schlegel was motivated by nationalistic feelings and the desire to prevent the further spread of French influence, whether cultural or military. The earlier cosmopolitan, who had praised Germany chiefly as a *Kulturnation,* was now in closer sympathy with the fervent patriotism of the philosopher Fichte. A brief visit to his native Hanover, reduced to a provincial role in the newly-created Kingdom of Westphalia under Napoleon's brother, Jerome, convinced Schlegel that the time for theorizing was over, and that practical measures were called for if his country were to be liberated.

Annoyances and frequent altercations with his strong-willed patroness characterized the next four years. Madame de Staël, although hostile towards Napoleon, was very much a product of French culture, notwithstanding her new-found enthusiasm for German life and literature. Schlegel, though often consulted in the preparation of *De l'Allemagne,* became acutely aware that many of his anti-French biases were simply being toned down or ignored by its authoress. In April 1810 Madame de Staël and her retinue established themselves in the castle of Chaumont-sur-Loire to await the publication of the work in Tours. Suddenly, the arbitrary weight of Napoleon's censorship descended, and the printing plates and all copies of the book already run off were ordered to be destroyed. Madame de Staël and Schlegel were peremptorily expelled from the country and restricted to the confines of Coppet. Later in 1814 Schlegel saw the original order of expulsion in Paris which stated that "a certain M. Chelègue [sic], a longtime house companion of Madame de Staël, is anti-Napoleon, anti-French, in one word German-minded, and must therefore no longer be endured in France." No doubt he regarded this testament to his ability to infuriate Napoleon with the greatest of satisfaction.

In 1810 Madame de Staël's friend, General Bernadotte, had become the Swedish Crown Prince. Gradually the idea of escaping to England via a circuitous northern route, thus avoiding the danger of arrest in France or Germany, began to form in her mind. The situation at Coppet had noticeably worsened; Madame de Staël was virtually under house arrest, and Schlegel reduced to the surreptitious role of messenger, spiriting away a clandestine copy of *De l'Allemagne* to Vienna as well as obtaining passports through a mixture of guile and diplomacy for his employer and her new, but still secret, husband. On May 23, 1812, the long-planned flight began, and after a bad scare in Salzburg and a later delay in Vienna while awaiting Russian passports, the tired travellers reached Moscow, only five weeks before the city was consumed by flames. In St. Petersburg Schlegel took the opportunity to discuss the political future of Germany with the statesman Freiherr vom Stein; according to Ernst Moritz Arndt, another patriot in exile and an eyewitness to the meeting, Schlegel could not resist dressing up in his best finery, wearing snow-white silk hose and shoes with golden buckles which gave him the appearance of a French abbé. Whatever the circumstances, he was to remain the *Hofmann* throughout life.

It was soon after the group's arrival in Stockholm that Schlegel embarked on a brief activist political career. Thanks to a recommendation from Madame de Staël before she sailed for England, he became Bernadotte's adviser and secretary. The immediate result was his *"Mémoire sur l'état de l'Allemagne et sur les moyens d'y former une insurrection nationale"* in which he advocated attacking Napoleon from the rear while his army was far away in Russia. Schlegel pointed out the danger of Germany being squeezed from both sides should the French return victorious; this could only be prevented by a resurgence of the German Empire under a *"grand capitaine,"* indicating that Bernadotte was the man of the hour. Schlegel envisioned vom Stein as Chancellor and a Reichstag composed of patriotic princes and the most suitable men in Germany. A new Hanseatic navy would join with Sweden to ward off France, who would herself benefit by becoming a constitutional monarchy. The Constitution of the Empire was to be rewritten, with the princes acknowledging the preeminence of the Kaiser. Only two problems remained: vom Stein was implacably hostile to the princes and wanted them to abdicate, and Austria was now allied by family ties to France.

In his private correspondence of this period Schlegel reveals himself as considerably less optimistic about Germany's future. Equating his own personal disappointments with those of his country, he wrote to Madame de Staël's son, Auguste:

> After having experienced so many bitter lessons [*"desengaños"* in the original letter] in my life, first of all in love, then in friendship, finding myself isolated in declining age without any other fortune than a modest literary fame, I still feel myself animated by a single desire, that of inscribing my name honorably in the shameful history of my homeland. If I fail there as in everything else, it will be time to withdraw from the world and to write to one another: vanitas, vanitatum!

But the distinct possibility of peace, that would enable Napoleon to regroup and again seize the military initiative, caused Schlegel to despair of Germany's future. Comparing himself somewhat fancifully to King David, he surveyed the fragmented German scene with dismay and defiance.

In February 1813 Schlegel wrote his *"Sur le système continental,"* detailing the detrimental effects to all countries of the economic blockade against England. As a result of Napoleon's stubbornness and shortsightedness, he maintained, food prices had risen with consequent impoverishment, armies were willing to turn on civilians, and the war against Russia was little more than a "crusade against coffee and sugar." In another pamphlet, *"Betrachtungen über die Politik der danischen Regierung"*— Schlegel apparently wrote in whatever language best suited his purposes—he supported the Swedish position by criticizing Denmark's treatment of its German subjects in Holstein and for having allied itself with Napoleon. As a reward for his articulate works he was made a Swedish Privy Councillor and given the Vasa order; he now styled himself "Chevalier" and von Schlegel, complete with a coat-of-arms and a family crest bearing the name of Schlegel von Gottleben. At the same time, he procured a horse at the Swedish headquarters in Stralsund, a medieval knight anxious to take part in battle. Apparently the poor animal was lacking in martial qualities, preferring the sanctuary of the baggage train to the battlefield of Leipzig (October 16-18, 1813). Schlegel lamely explained, *"J'enrage de ne m'être pas pourvu à temps d'un bon cheval"* ("I'm furious at not having provided myself in time with a good horse") and picked up his pen again.

Now that Napoleon had been routed, it was only a matter of time before the Allies would be in Paris. This in turn raised the issue of the succession. Napoleon had earlier written an article in the *Leipziger Zeitung* in which he had unintentionally honored Schlegel by singling him out for special criticism. The latter's reply was a parallel study comparing Buonaparte with tyrants such as Tiberius and Nero, and extolling Bernadotte as a reincarnation of Henri IV (both came from Gascony and,

incidentally, changed their religion for political purposes).
In his romantic imagination Schlegel even visualized a
duel between the two leaders with God and Gustavus
Adolphus looking down from heaven to ensure victory for
the righteous! Surprisingly enough, Bernadotte thought
that Schlegel's style lacked fire, though he was secretly
flattered by the thought that he might ascend the throne
of his native land.

The winter of 1813 and the following spring were
months of personal setbacks. At the very moment that
the allied armies crossed into France, Schlegel fell ill with
pneumonia and was incapacitated for several weeks. His
recovery was not hastened by the news that Madame de
Staël had completely failed to take into account the new
sense of national unity in Germany in the revision of her
preface to *De l'Allemagne*. Nor were his spirits lifted
when it appeared that practically everyone else possessed
a copy of the newly-published book except the man responsible for so much of the basic research. Furthermore,
Madame de Staël, with a singular lack of foresight, had
never entertained the possibility that her beloved France
might have to be occupied by foreign armies in order to
unseat Napoleon. The advance of the Germans and Russians toward Paris filled her with despair; her earlier
pro-German sentiments were now forgotten.

Already in February 1813 the future Louis XVIII
had issued a public proclamation from England announc-
ing his policies should he be called upon to rule over
France. The tone was conciliatory: the majority of officials would retain their positions, and the *Code Napoléon*
would continue as the law of the land. Faced with this
generous spirit, Schlegel had to tread warily in his
*"Analyse de la proclamation de Louis XVIII aux Fran-
çais,"* written on Bernadotte's behalf. His main argument
was that Louis could only offer his royal birth, a concept

97

rejected by the French in a plebiscite, that he was unknown to his people, and that his very candidacy denied that the Revolution had taken place. Schlegel's criticism was too sharp, and, significantly, his refutation was never published. Bernadotte, sensing that the French prize had slipped from his grasp, sought solace in the annexation of Norway from Denmark. The restoration of the Bourbons in effect marks the end of Schlegel's political career.

It is a curious fact that the translator of Calderón and Shakespeare had completed his great work without visiting the homelands of the two great dramatists. Schlegel never set foot in Spain during his entire life, but the climactic events of early 1814 gave him the opportunity to rejoin Madame de Staël in England after a year's separation. Little is know of his sojourn in London other than a description of the erstwhile privy councillor appearing at mid-morning elegantly dressed in his silk dressing-gown and slippers. In May the two weary, middle-aged literati established themselves in Paris, and though *De l'Allemagne* was discussed and dissected in every salon, neither of them could summon the enthusiasm of previous years. Both were glad to return to Coppet where Schlegel could immerse himself again among his books in his *"chambre bleue."*

The *débâcle* at Waterloo and the final return of the Bourbons, soon to be followed by the death of Madame de Staël in 1817, extinguished any remaining political aspirations. At first Czar Alexander's Holy Alliance raised romantic hopes; but Metternich's prevailing influence in Germany and the stern reaction following the assassination of Kotzebue, a popular German dramatist suspected of being a Russian spy, resulted in the abandonment of more progressive policies.

Schlegel accepted the position of professor at the University of Bonn, and in addition to his pioneering work in the study of Sanskrit found time to write an occasional patriotic poem or political parody aimed at the French, often written in that language. Even so, the petty censorship at the university restricted his writings with the result that his remaining years—he lived to be seventy-eight—were spent in a demeaning succession of bitter arguments, imagined slights and caustic epigrams. The ironic award of the cross of the *Légion d'honneur* in 1831 from the hands of Louis Philippe did little to mollify him; he was soon angered by French claims to the left bank of the Rhine. He retained a suspicion and dislike of French policies until the day of his death in 1845. The last years were lonely ones, and Schlegel had lived long enough to see Madame de Staël's three children, whom he had tutored, precede him to the grave.

Schlegel's life and attitudes were a curious intermingling of the cosmopolitan and the nationalistic. Unfortunately, the breadth of scholarship was never transmuted into a corresponding breadth of political vision. He failed to recognize the true import of the French Revolution or to distinguish between Napoleon the man and Napoleon the harbinger of a new era. It has been remarked that hostilities between nations often result not from an absence of information about a neighboring country but from a superabundance. Certainly few men knew more about French life and culture than did Schlegel, whose original works in that language bear testimony to his close involvement. While one may praise unsullied patriotism, Schlegel's attitudes were tainted by preconceived judgments. What was lacking was not knowledge, but a generosity of spirit; his arrogance and pretensions to nobility blinded him to much that Napoleon had instituted in Germany, and in this respect Goethe, the born aristocrat, was more perceptive. Ultimately Schlegel—linguist, historian, critic, scholar, and part-time politician—understood every age, all, that is, except his own.

Clemens Metternich

"It was only in Paris that my public life began," we are told in the Austrian statesman's *Memoirs,* those self-justifying tomes that by now must strike the reader as *de rigeur.* They cover a long career and a vast terrain, but, as in the case of Chateaubriand, the years of contiguity with Napoleon are the heart of the narrative. In his excellent biography, Alan Palmer characterizes the nostalgia of Metternich's old age as he regaled his listeners with reminiscences of past meetings with the Emperor:

> ... he saw himself time and time again at the Tuileries or St. Cloud, sharpening phrases he had almost used, recounting compliments the Emperor failed to offer.... Countess Lieven, listening to Metternich for the first time in 1818, was delighted by his tales of the fallen Emperor; and we find them still talking of him when

they meet thirty years later. It is as if Napoleon, even in death, overshadowed the Chancellor of Europe. And here is the most curious paradox of Metternich's career. For, vainest of statesmen though he was, he never sensed such distinction in the epoch to which historians appropriated his name as in the reflected glory of Napoleon's empire.

Though Metternich remained in power until the revolutions of 1848, the thirty-three years that followed Waterloo are an extended epilogue as increasingly he became an aging anachronism. His success was that of cunning survival, a wary conservative in an age of ferment, for whom the principle of legitimacy and the balance of power stood in valiant contrast to the liberal evils that beset him on all sides. If stability secured peace, the corollary was that radical change caused wars and must therefore be avoided at all costs. This, in essence, was Metternich's system during the greater part of his life, yet one senses that secretly he was bored with it all; he himself admitted: "The one giant whom the eighteenth century produced is no longer of this world; all the stir of today is made by men of pitiable stamp. It is hard indeed to play well with such poor actors." The "coachman of Europe," as Metternich became known, would gladly have turned the reins over to others for the chance to match wits once more with the Emperor who long since had become a legend.

The young Clemens Metternich, born in Coblenz in 1773, grew up in that same Rhineland that nurtured Konrad Adenauer a century later. Though Austrian by birth, his early years were spent on the periphery of the Empire, much closer to French influence than the imperial capital of Vienna. His father was a Councillor of State, a landed aristocrat and convinced conservative who watched the revolutionary rumblings across the Rhine with dismay. Clemens, sent to the University of Strasbourg at the age of fifteen, approved the ease with which a local riot was put down; even as a youth he felt that such nonsense must be nipped in the bud. The Coronation of Leopold II in 1790 as Holy Roman Emperor at Frankfurt was a more congenial event, representing, to all outward appearances at least, the sanction of centuries. The young man continued his legal studies at the University of Mainz at a time when the city was rapidly filling with émigrés intent on forming an army to invade revolutionary France. In March 1792, Leopold died, to be succeeded by his twenty-four-year-old son, Francis. Clemens was but nineteen at the time of the Coronation of the new Emperor, whom he was later to serve for a third of a century.

The early revolutionary wars did not affect Metternich initially, being still fought in the casual eighteenth-century manner that Napoleon would change so decisively. In 1794 the aspiring diplomat was sent to London on a special mission, followed by a frustrating experience in Holland trying to locate an elusive government in the face of advancing French armies. Clearly the Hapsburg territories in the Netherlands were lost, and soon the revolutionary armies were in occupation of the Rhineland, including Coblenz. The Metternichs, father and son, were criticized freely for alleged ineptitude, and it must have been with apprehension that Clemens saw Vienna for the first time in November 1794. The only way for the family to recoup its reputation and income, both diminished by French occupation, was through an alliance to a prestigious family. Clemens' marriage to Eleonore von Kaunitz, granddaughter of Maria Theresa's illustrious Chancellor, was a brilliant maneuver on the part of Madame Metternich; the wedding was celebrated in September 1795 on the Kaunitz estate at Austerlitz, the scene of a far less joyous event ten years later.

Bonaparte's sensational victories against the Austrian armies in northern Italy had resulted in the harsh treaties of Leoben and Campo Formio and the loss of imperial territories to France. A Congress at Rastatt was summoned which both Metternichs, now partially back in favor, attended in their capacity as staunch guardians of established interests. The French delegation was supposed to have been led by General Bonaparte; he failed to appear, having more pressing matters to attend to in Egypt. The Congress dragged on inconclusively, and the face-to-face meeting of Napoleon and Metternich was delayed for a further eight years. By 1799 Austria was again at war with France, and though the first months were marked by the recovery of many of the lost Italian territories, Bonaparte's victory at Marengo and Moreau's triumph at Hohenlinden forced Emperor Francis to negotiate with his adversary, now risen to First Consul and master of France. Meanwhile, Metternich was appointed Austrian Minister to the Court of Saxony at Dresden, a pleasant enough position, but with modest prospects.

Life at the baroque court was undemanding, unimaginative and, as a consequence, unsatisfying to one with higher ambitions. A succession of children was born to the young couple, but already Metternich had acquired the first of the many mistresses who accompanied his own three marriages. The faithful and forgiving Eleonore stood by while he collected beautiful ladies with an ease that was the envy of Europe; they ranged from the wife of a Russian general to Napoleon's sister Caroline, admittedly an easy conquest. On an occasion when otherwise occupied, Metternich made the acquaintance of Friedrich Gentz, an erratic political genius and dedicated enemy of Napoleon. In early 1803 Metternich was transferred to Berlin, but combining native indolence with diplomatic leisureliness, he arrived in the Prussian capital late in November. The following year he attended Madame de Staël's salon, having earlier listened to the public lectures of August Wilhelm Schlegel. The news of the murder of the duc d'Enghien and the elevation of Napoleon to Emperor outraged the born aristocrat. He was opposed to granting diplomatic recognition of the imperial title to Napoleon, as such recognition would confirm the upstart's entrée to the select family of reigning monarchs; his view was overruled, and the presence of the Pope at the coronation in December terminated the matter.

Soon Metternich became the distant spectator to a tragic event that he was unable to influence, much less control. Austria, in alliance with the Russia of Czar Alexander, judged the moment suitable in 1805 to strike decisively against the French, if at all possible in conjunction with an attack by the Prussians in the north. Metternich failed completely in his efforts to convince King Frederick William that intervention was vital; undaunted, Austria gambled on a swift campaign, only to suffer the successive disasters of Ulm and Austerlitz. To complete her humiliation, Austria lost further territories and had to pay a huge indemnity. Within a few months, the Holy Roman Empire was laid to rest with Napoleon performing the last rites, and Francis reduced to the more realistic rank of Emperor of Austria. This turn of events necessitated a new Austrian ambassador in Paris; Napoleon made some flattering allusions to the memory of Kaunitz, the hint was debated at length in Vienna, and Metternich, thanks to his wife's family connections, was appointed to the post. His public life in the highest councils had now begun.

The first meeting between Metternich and the French Emperor took place at St. Cloud on August 10, 1806. The occasion was the presentation of the new ambassador's diplomatic credentials, and already there is latent conflict between patrician and self-proclaimed Emperor. With the coloration of hindsight, Metternich has left us the following description of their first encounter:

> I found him standing in the middle of one of the *salons* with the Minister of Foreign Affairs and six other members of the Court. He was wearing the uniform of the Guard and kept his hat on. This latter detail, unbecoming in every respect because the audience was not public, struck me as being a misplaced pretension and smacking of the *parvenu....* His build was short and square, a careless appearance, but yet an attempt to make himself look imposing which resulted in weakening in me the feeling of grandeur which naturally one attaches to the man who used to make the earth shake.

As frequently in the *Memoirs,* the account digresses from the descriptive to the philosophical:

> This impression has never been completely erased from my mind; it has been with me in the most important meetings that I had with Napoleon at different times of his career. It is possible that it helped show me the man as he really was beyond the masks he used to hide behind. In his outbursts, his temper tantrums, his brusque interruptions, I became used to seeing as many prepared scenes, studied and calculated in their effect, as he wished to produce on his listener.

If Metternich was not overawed by his adversary, neither does it seem that Napoleon was at first greatly impressed by a man he regarded deficient in experience and perception. The events of the coming years were to dispel these mutual misjudgments.

During the next year the two men saw very little of one another. Prussia insisted on imitating Austria's recent sorrowful example and was duly routed at Auerstadt and Jena, thus supporting Metternich's contention that it was division among the allies opposing France that produced defeat rather than any supposed superiority of Napoleon.

Metternich was quick to perceive that the French Empire was an imposing façade whose foundations rested on the shoulders of one man, and that, conversely, the policies of Talleyrand and Fouché—no matter how devious and unprincipled the practitioners—represented more of a European outlook and thus a securer base for the future. These considerations did not divert him from profitable affairs with Napoleon's sister Caroline, married to Murat (soon to be King of Naples), and with the wife of General Junot—after all, these highly placed ladies also had access to useful information. Such amorous liaisons, Metternich must have felt, were but a pleasurable extension of Clausewitz' famous dictum that war was but a continuation of politics.

Much that was taking place was beyond Metternich's ability to change or influence; he was still serving his diplomatic apprenticeship in a clearly deferential relationship to the French Emperor. The meeting with the Czar at Tilsit in 1807, the forced abdication of the Spanish Bourbons at Bayonne a year later, and the imposing gathering of the monarchs at Erfurt all took place without his participation, though Talleyrand, whose sympathies tended to be pro-Austrian, provided him detailed descriptions of what had transpired. The Austrian army was undergoing much-needed reforms, and the defeat of a French army at Bailén in 1808 at the hands of Spanish patriots had provided new encouragement to fight another war. Napoleon took advantage of a diplomatic occasion (his own birthday) to stage one of his famous scenes. The various accounts differ in detail, especially as to whether Napoleon raved at Metternich or kept his composure. The opening broadside was a pointed question: "Well, and is Austria arming on a large scale?" followed by a harangue that lasted over an hour, clearly aimed at intimidating and embarrassing the Austrian ambassador in the presence of his colleagues. Metternich supposedly retorted that "if you have counted our soldiers, we have counted yours"; in any event, Napoleon became more conciliatory, and a few days later even attempted to patch up the quarrel. Both then and later there was no lasting rancor between the two adversaries; each had taken the measure of the other and found much to respect.

Now, in 1809, Metternich made a major miscalculation. He had indeed counted the soldiers on both sides, and having concluded that Napoleon was hopelessly embroiled in Spain, supported the group in Vienna that favored a war of revenge. The gamble nearly succeeded, and had the Austrian army movements been better coordinated and concentrated at the critical moment, Napoleon might well have been beaten. As it was, the gory battle of Aspern and Essling was a reciprocal slaughter that ended in a stalemate, and Napoleon's costly victory at Wagram was certainly no disaster on the level of Austerlitz. Once again, though, Austria had to accept defeat and the occupation of Vienna, but the war portended a radical change in Napoleon's fortunes; the era of easy victories was at an end.

During the early stages of the war, Metternich continued his diplomatic mission in Paris unmolested, even after Napoleon's departure to assume command of the army. Not until the battle of Aspern did he make his dignified departure from Paris, interrupting a leisurely journey to Vienna to pay his respects to the Empress Josephine at Strasbourg. Technically, he was a prisoner of the French, but this did not prevent his watching the battle of Wagram at a safe distance through a telescope, in the best tradition of the eighteenth century. Metternich was held partially responsible for Austria's predicament and took little part in the peace talks that followed, especially as he now favored a rapprochement with France, a policy distasteful to Emperor Francis and other patriots. Nevertheless, there was an urgent need to fill the post of Foreign Minister; Metternich was available, *faute de mieux,* and was appointed to the position that Kaunitz had held with such distinction for thirty-nine years. At the moment of national humiliation, few would have wagered that this mannered statesman would raise Austria to new heights and become the dominant figure in Europe until mid-century.

Metternich's intimate relationship with Caroline Murat had convinced him that Napoleon was giving considerable thought to a possible divorce from Josephine. She had failed to provide him with a male heir, and two of his mistresses had presented him with tangible proof of his potency. If Austria's immediate fate was to remain subservient to France, then why not secure Napoleon's attachment through a dynastic alliance? From personal experience Metternich knew all about advantageous marriages and regarded the eighteen-year old Marie Louise, daughter of Emperor Francis, as perfectly suited. His task was simplified when Czar Alexander refused to countenance a union between his youngest sister and the upstart Corsican, having neither forgotten nor forgiven the murder of the duc d'Enghien, a prince of the blood.

Apparently it was Napoleon himself who initiated discussions with Metternich's wife at a masked ball. Eleonore had little difficulty piercing the Emperor's transparent disguise, and the message was passed on to Vienna. Notwithstanding Francis' justifiable misgivings—the recent war, Napoleon's questionable past, and the whole matter of the divorce—he reluctantly gave in, and the first marriage ceremony (by proxy) took place in Vienna. Napoleon rode as far as Compiègne to greet the bridal party on its journey to Paris; when Cardinal Fesch, that obliging family cleric, assured his nephew that the marriage was already legitimate, no time was wasted in securing the succession to the throne. When, a few days later, Metternich indiscreetly proposed a toast to the "King of Rome" (the title of Napoleon's future son had already been announced), not a diplomatic eyebrow was raised.

The six months spent in Paris during the summer of 1810 enabled Metternich to gain a deeper insight into the workings of Napoleon's mind. The marriage to Marie Louise was a success, not merely due to her early pregnancy but, more surprisingly, to a genuine bond of affection between the partners of this political union. In later life Metternich boasted that he had come to know Napoleon better than any non-Frenchman, yet during his weeks of personal contact he often contradicted his own assessment of the Emperor. No doubt wishing to assume reflected credit for his own diplomacy, he assured Marie Louise's father of the beneficial influence she wielded over her husband. Yet towards the end of July we find Metternich informing his Emperor that "the aspiration to universal power is in the very nature of Napoleon; it can be modified and checked, but one will never succeed in stifling it." Such lingering fears in no way prevented Metternich and Napoleon from enjoying one another's company and exchanging minor confidences; when the Foreign Minister finally set out for Vienna in September, laden with gifts and complimentary letters, he must have felt well-satisfied with his astute diplomacy.

As his carriage rolled eastwards, Metternich had ample time to reflect on his relationship with the French Emperor and his own ambivalent feelings toward him. In his *Memoirs*, impressions and vignettes are interwoven to form a fascinating portrait. Metternich praises the perspicacity of Napoleon's mind, his ability to get to the crux of the matter. We are told that he had no trouble in telling the Emperor the truth, even if it proved displeasing. It seems that Napoleon felt no reverse obligation, telling Metternich in a candid moment that he regarded Parisians as children to be lied to in the official bulletins: "I'm not writing them for you; the Parisians believe everything, and I could tell them quite a few other things they would not resist accepting." Napoleon regretted his lack of regal legitimacy, but protested that he was not a usurper, as he had found the throne vacant; indeed, he was the new Charlemagne, having created a new Empire. He felt called upon to follow his destiny, which was that of France, indissolubly bound together and guided by the same star.

Metternich has left us an engaging glimpse of Napoleon in a domestic setting. In company he was often self-consciously aware of his squat stature and over-compensated by strutting around in a poor imitation of the Bourbons or his actor friend Talma. Within his own family, he was like an extremely good-natured Italian father, even taking orders from Marie Louise. His views on family life were strictly traditional, and Metternich notes that at receptions he would ask women as a matter of course how many children they had and whether they breastfed them (it would seem that Mme de Staël had not been singled out for special embarrassment during that disastrous interview). Metternich notes: "His feeling towards women mixing in politics or administration he carried to the point of hatred," but in a general appraisal —surprisingly similar to Mme de Staël's—he notes:

> Napoleon had two fronts. As a private citizen he was easy to get along with, being neither good nor wicked. As a statesman, he did not allow any feeling to enter in, deciding neither by affection nor hatred. He pushed aside

or crushed his enemies, without consulting anything else except the need or interest to get rid of them. Having reached his aim, he forgot them and did not persecute them.

Metternich had reason to feel apprehensive upon his arrival in Vienna. He had been absent for over half a year, and what he termed diplomacy was condemned by patriotic Austrians as collaboration with an enemy that had waged war three times in the space of fifteen years and whose future actions were entirely unpredictable. He was convinced that war between France and Russia had become inevitable; the Czar had rejected the Continental System, thus allowing English goods to enter the mainland again, and at the beginning of 1811 France annexed the Duchy of Oldenburg, whose ruler was married to the Czar's favorite sister. Nor had the Polish situation been resolved despite (or perhaps because of) repeated divisions of that hapless land. It would naturally be in Austria's vital interest to remain neutral in such a cataclysmic struggle, but Metternich was certain that Napoleon would never consent to his father-in-law's remaining uninvolved. Thanks to some adroit moves on Metternich's part, Austria provided a token army corps of thirty thousand men under its own commander, which enabled it to survive the Russian campaign almost intact —a nonfeat of arms that made the French Emperor furious.

Pride preceded his fall in like proportions. The convocation of kings and princes at Dresden during the latter part of May 1812 was accompanied by pageantry and festivities that gave little hint of the coming tragedy on the frozen Russian plains. The Austrian royal couple still could not bring themselves to enthuse over their powerful son-in-law, but Metternich and Napoleon resumed the pleasant inconsequential confidences of the previous year.

Once again the subject of the Austrian contribution to the campaign was briefly mentioned, but Metternich parried the thrust with suitable evasive assurances. The conversations might well have ended on an acrimonious note had Napoleon got wind of Metternich's intimation to Czar Alexander that the Austrian forces would be non-combatants as far as possible.

The news of the disaster in Russia changed Austria's position from that of reluctant ally to an armed neutral. Metternich's position as a mediator was greatly strengthened, and the safe return of the unscathed army corps underlined Austria's growing military power. His devious success won him little popularity at home, where the patriotic mood favored a grand alliance to overthrow the hated French Emperor. Francis still had scruples about attacking his formidable relative and together with his Foreign Minister viewed with mistrust any call for a popular uprising as potentially dangerous and uncontrollable. A chastened Napoleon was regarded as a necessary counterbalance to the unpredictable Czar, with Austria playing the dominant neutral role in central Europe. Such a policy required a lasting peace settlement, but any such hopes were shattered by the alliance between Russia and Prussia, and soon Napoleon had crossed the Rhine at the head of an army of young conscripts. Two narrow French victories left both sides exhausted and in desperate need of a truce; Metternich saw the opportunity to mediate between the Czar and Napoleon, and believed that the six-weeks' armistice might perhaps be extended into a permanent peace treaty. This would require considerable sacrifice on his part, as the summer of 1813 had produced a most delectable crop of mistresses he was loathe to leave.

In the meantime, Czar Alexander had become imbued with a religious fervor that transmuted the war against Napoleon into a crusade against the anti-Christ. In such a mood he extracted a commitment from Metternich that Austria would join the Allies should peace talks with the French fail to reach a satisfactory agreement by July 20. Metternich's subsequent meeting with Napoleon at Dresden has become the subject of intense debate among historians; only the two men were present, and the main account is Metternich's suspect version written several years afterwards. Did he negotiate in good faith or was he, as French critics insist, presenting Napoleon with an ultimatum knowing that war was inevitable? Were the peace terms offered reasonable or were they designed to humiliate the French Emperor?

The decisive meeting took place in the Marcolini Palace outside Dresden on June 26. Quickly dispensing with formalities, Napoleon immediately assailed the surprised Metternich with a prepared attack: "So you, too, want war; well, you shall have it! I have annihilated the Prussian army at Lützen; I have beaten the Russians at Bautzen; now you wish your turn to come. So be it; we shall meet in Vienna. Men are incorrigible: experience is lost upon you. Three times I have replaced the Emperor Francis on his throne. I have promised always to live in peace with him; I have married his daughter. At the same time I said to myself 'You are perpetrating a folly'; but it was done, and today I regret it."

If the latter remark was intended to disconcert Metternich by alluding to his responsibility in the marriage, it failed completely. Unperturbed, the minister reminded Napoleon that only by retiring to France's natural borders could peace be assured. The indignant Emperor's reply is a revealing self-portrait of a man driven by inner forces he can no longer control: "Well then, what do people want me to do? To degrade myself? Never! I shall know how to die, but I shall not surrender one inch of soil. Rulers who are born to the throne can be defeated twenty times and always return to their capitals; but I, a child of fortune, cannot; my reign will not outlast the day I cease to be strong and people no longer fear me." Napoleon conceded that the Russian winter had demoralized his generals, who now desired peace, but his soldiers were as brave as ever and under his generalship would go on to victory.

Metternich remained uncowed and retorted: "Fortune may deceive you a second time, as it did in 1812. In ordinary times armies comprise only a small part of the population, today it is the whole people you have called to arms. Is not your present army formed by anticipating a generation? I have seen your soldiers; they are mere children." Napoleon, livid with rage, turned on his tormentor with abuse that Metternich assures the reader had to be toned down before he could print it: "You are no soldier and you do not know what goes on in the mind of a soldier. I was brought up in the field, and a man such as I am does not concern himself much about the lives of a million men." With that he threw his hat into the corner of the room. Other accounts depict an irate Emperor snatching Metternich's hat from out of his hands, and Napoleon himself later claimed to have flung it down thirteen times with his antagonist dutifully retrieving it each time—not a convincing picture.

The confrontation lasted for over eight hours, during which the anxious generals outside the conference room remained transfixed by the gravity of the discussion. In between lengthy digressions, Metternich supposedly declared war some half dozen times, and again the matter of Napoleon's ill-advised marriage was dissected, culminating in the truculent observation that "when I married an Archduchess, I tried to weld the new with the old, Gothic prejudices with the institutions of my century: I deceived myself, and I, this day, feel the whole extent of my error. It may cost me my throne, but I will bury the world beneath its ruins." Metternich saw that his mission had failed, and turning once more to the Emperor before taking leave told him: "You are lost, Sire. I had the presentiment of it when I came; now, in going, I have the certainty."

Though Metternich had called Napoleon *"un homme perdu,"* there was one further meeting between the two at which they agreed to extend the armistice and continue peace talks in Prague. It was the last occasion on which they met, and both knew that any further discussions were but a respite before war was resumed. Napoleon's position as a "child of fortune" did not allow for compromise, nor could he resist the gamble of the last victory that would scatter his enemies and enable him to return in triumph. But at Leipzig his good fortune deserted him as the combined allied army forced him to retreat eastwards; two days later, a grateful Emperor Francis made Metternich a Prince of the Austrian Empire.

The winter campaign of 1813-14 that ensued was characterized as much by allied discord and suspicion as by any outstanding strategy in the field. Napoleon proved himself a master tactician in retreat, and time and again threw the advancing armies off balance, only withdrawing in the face of overwhelming numbers. Metternich was anxious to preserve a viable Napoleonic France east of the Rhine that was capable of counterbalancing the emergence of Prussia and particularly of Russia. With this long-range aim in mind, he was prepared to offer Napoleon generous peace terms, fully aware that such a move would incur the hostility of the Czar, bent on revenging the destruction of Moscow. At one point Metternich visualized a regency under Marie Louise as a possible compromise solution, but Napoleon's stubbornness and sudden collapse foredoomed any such idea. In vain he protested the choice of the island of Elba for the deposed Emperor's exile, prophesying the renewed outbreak of war within two years, but the selection of Vienna as the site for peace deliberations helped mollify his exasperation.

With considerable tact, Metternich stayed away from Paris to enable the vainglorious Czar to savor a triumphant entry, relying on adulation and Talleyrand to save the city from any bitter reprisal by the allies. Once the Bourbons were safely back, the diplomatic caravan crossed over to London to continue the festivities and postwar discussions. The Czar without much trouble irritated the Prince Regent, greatly to the satisfaction of Metternich, who found the company of Cardinal Consalvi, the Pope's confidant, far more congenial. By mid-summer Metternich was back in Vienna, where the Congress was due to begin on October 1 with Gentz as its secretary. No number of social events could conceal the enmity between the participants—and Metternich suffered the added mortification of losing his Russian mistress to the Czar. The frequent disagreements—even talk of a new war—spread gloom about the future, except on the island of Elba. The Emperor Francis had refused to permit Marie Louise to join her husband in exile, and after an enforced residence at the Schönbrunn Palace, consented to his daughter taking the waters at Aix-les-Bains. As added protection he sent a cavalry general to watch over her; within a few weeks they were lovers.

During the winter of 1814-15 the bickering and balls continued, to the consternation of the Viennese. Talleyrand caustically observed that the sovereigns were "too frightened to fight one another, too stupid to agree." Napoleon decided matters for them. Metternich felt in retrospect that the Hundred Days was a terrible mistake, deploring especially the liberal pose adopted by the desperate Emperor:

> In a hundred days Bonaparte undid the work of the fourteen years during which he had been in power. He let loose the revolution which he had suppressed in France. He brought men's minds back, not to the 18th of Brumaire, but to the principles which had been adopted by the Constituent Assembly in its deplorable blindness.

For France, the three months that ended at Waterloo resulted in the imposition of far more severe measures than the lenient terms of 1814. The usual haggling among the allies went on interminably, but for Metternich an era was ended and a new one was about to begin.

Though the most powerful man in Europe until ousted by the 1848 revolution, Metternich never aspired to become Emperor. A realist, he held to the tenet that power must be exercised judiciously to be truly effective. Up to his death in 1859 at the age of eighty-six, he was informally consulted by royalty and statesmen. His career had none of the *éclat* that surrounded Napoleon, but then it lasted three times as long.

While the French Emperor had been rendered harmless in his Atlantic fastness, there was a constant reminder of his presence in Vienna. His son, the Duke of Reichstadt, was also the grandson of the Emperor Francis, who took a keen interest in educating him as a Hapsburg prince. Both Metternich and Marie Louise chose to ignore him as far as possible, and it was only when "the Eaglet" reached manhood that the Prince saw him as a possible political pawn. By then it was too late, tuberculosis had set in, and a premature end came at Schönbrunn Palace on July 22, 1832.

At the news of Napoleon's death in 1821, Metternich is supposed to have remarked: "This accident is no longer an event." Happily, this casual quip was not his final word on the man with whom he had dueled so often. Later, in a more reflective mood, he wrote:

> He was born a conqueror, legislator and administrator, and thought he could follow this triple path at the same time; his undeniable genius provided him with the means. The opinion of the great majority of the nation would have been satisfied had he limited himself to the cares of government.

It was self-advice that Metternich took to heart.

Manuel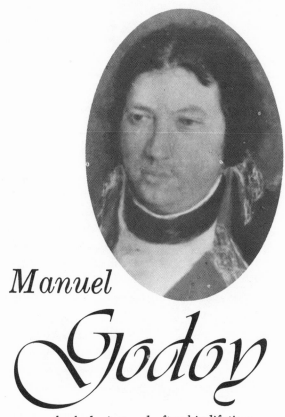

Godoy

Rarely has a man, both during and after his lifetime, been so generally vilified by an entire nation as has Manuel Godoy, *"el Príncipe de la Paz."* Hardly an historian or novelist has failed to blame the Prince of the Peace for Spain's misfortunes during the Napoleonic period, holding him personally responsible for the country's poor state of military preparedness as well as the scandalous immoral behavior at Court. Godoy still remains the classic scapegoat, despite more recent attempts to achieve a truer perspective. Most descriptions are content to dwell on his supposed exploits with the Queen in the royal bedroom, emphasizing his personal accumulation of wealth and titles but denying him any redeeming qualities. In fact, the great nineteenth-century Spanish critic Menéndez y Pelayo even claimed that Godoy was demonstrably incapable of writing his own *Memorias!*

In sum, he is scornfully dismissed as the *parvenu* among *privados*, the ruin of his country, entirely lacking in morals, ability, or integrity.

Godoy was born in Badajoz in western Spain on May 12, 1767, of Christian aristocratic stock that claimed direct lineage from the Visigoths. His father came from Estremadura, the land of Cortés, Pizarro, and Balboa, and his mother, as befits the city's frontier position, was of Portuguese origin. The youth's education seems to have been surprisingly thorough and filled with the generous spirit of the French Enlightenment. In his later years in exile he would boast of his cultural achievements while in office and of having befriended many of the leading writers and artists of his day. His amazing rise to power, however, was less due to any intellectual ability than to his elder brother Luis having prepared the way at Court as a young guardsman and, it was rumored, as lover of the future Queen.

Whatever the reason, Godoy soon had the good fortune to attract the attention of the Prince of Asturias, the future King Charles IV, and more especially that of his sensual wife, María Luisa. The oft-repeated anecdote of Godoy's fall from his horse at the Princess' feet and then having impressed her with his courage upon remounting his charger is regrettably based on the flimsiest of facts; his rapid promotion and easy access to the royal couple is not. From this time onward until the death in 1819 of the elderly dethroned monarchs, within a few days of one another, Manuel (as he was familiarly called) was to form the vital element of the *Santa Trinidad,* the caustic nickname given the ruling trio by their enemies.

In 1788 the austere Charles III was laid to rest and his son ascended the throne amid great initial enthusiasm. The new King and Queen had served an apprenticeship of twenty-three years, and were dismayed that part of their inheritance included two elderly statesmen who proffered unsolicited and contradictory advice. Count Aranda was not only a liberal Freemason and supposedly irreligious, but also supported many of the aims of the French Revolution. On the other hand, Count Florida-blanca was vacillating and hesitant, believing that the strict enforcement of new censorship laws would stem the rising revolutionary tide. To complicate matters further, the rival ministers and their followers detested each other, thereby dividing the Spanish Court into two hostile factions.

Charles IV was a kindly man but of weak character, more interested in the hunt and repairing watches than in the art of governing. In pursuit of these ingenuous ends he required a confidant who would be the King's own minister and unswervingly loyal, independent of all political groups. Such a man was Manuel Godoy. Whatever untruths may be contained in his *Memorias,* there seems little reason to doubt his own account of his rise to power:

> Troubled and uncertain in their power of decision, they [the royal couple] conceived the idea of finding a man and making him an incorruptible friend, the product of their own hands, one who would be closely united to the royal house and who would keep vigil over them and the kingdom without fail.

Incorruptible he certainly was not; but as a friend, he remained faithful to them in penurious exile unto death.

Godoy's dominant role in Spanish politics from 1792-1808 raises the question as to the true nature of his relationship with the Queen. A granddaughter of King Louis XV of France, María Luisa had been betrothed to her first cousin when she was only fourteen years old. Her married life was the traditional tragic cycle of accouchements—twenty-four pregnancies of which few children were to survive infancy. Tragically enough for Spain, one of those who did was the future Fernando VII, generally regarded as the worst king that Spain has been called upon to endure. Curiously, Godoy in later years was never held responsible as coprogenitor of this despot, but it was widely believed that he had fathered two of the surviving royal children. Contemporary descriptions and artistic likenesses frequently emphasized the striking resemblance between the Queen's favorite and the Infantes Francisco de Paula and María Isabel.

Many years later, María Luisa encouraged a possible match between her son and Godoy's legitimate daughter, Carlota, which, if the rumors were true, would have resulted in a consanguineous alliance that not even the inbreeding Spanish Bourbons would have countenanced. There seems little doubt that the Queen was indeed Godoy's royal mistress in every sense of the term, but it is also probable that María Luisa increasingly came to regard her Manuel, who was sixteen years younger, more as a son than a lover.

Godoy's accession to the rank of First Minister at the age of twenty-five can only be surpassed in precocity by that of his contemporary, William Pitt; even Bonaparte had to wait until thirty before making himself First Consul. When Count Aranda was dismissed in 1792, Godoy —recently created Duke of Alcudia—was given the immediate task of interceding on behalf of Louis XVI, a fellow Bourbon and Charles IV's first cousin. Despite much diplomatic maneuvering and an unrealistic offer of asylum in Spain, there was little that Godoy could do to save the French King's life. The revulsion felt in monarchist Spain against the godless regicides was easily fanned into popular enthusiasm for war with France, and even the smugglers in the Sierra Morena felt obliged to contribute funds to the crusade.

Godoy, who had been named a general in 1791 at the age of twenty-four (by contrast Bonaparte, two years his junior, had just been promoted to First Lieutenant), was acutely aware of the ill-preparedness of the Spanish army and privately counseled against hostilities. After some initial successes, the royal armies were thrown back onto Spanish soil by the French republican forces. The English and Spanish navies were forced to retire from Toulon in December 1793 due to the skillful use of artillery under Colonel Bonaparte's direction; shortly afterwards he was advanced to Brigadier-General. In Spain, disillusionment soon replaced the earlier optimism, and Godoy was only too anxious to begin peace negotiations in Basle. The resultant treaty was by no means unfavorable to Spain. A grateful sovereign showered honors on his young protégé, who received the impressive titles of "Prince of the Peace," "Knight of the Golden Fleece," and "Knight of Santiago," to name but a few. Even more remarkable, ignoring insinuations by Floridablanca and others as to the intimate relationship between the Queen and Godoy, the easy-going King fully shared his wife's affection for their "*querido* Manuel."

Most contemporary evaluations of the royal favorite reveal some degree of personal bias. He appears to have been about five feet, four inches tall, with regular features. Alcalá Galiano, who often saw Godoy at official receptions, mentions that he was "strongly made without corpulence, broad-shouldered, slightly bent, and very clear-complexioned." Goya's famous portrait is less kind, showing his subject in a general's uniform and tending to emphasize the fleshy, lustful nature of the man rather than the energetic administrator. The Prussian ambassador Rohde saw him as a combination of punctuality, hard work, and frivolity; and with good reason, for Godoy would frequently alleviate matters of state with affairs more congenial to his passionate nature, much to the Queen's mortification. The French ambassador, an accurate observer where beautiful women were concerned, sent back detailed dispatches to Paris relating the "heightened color and rumpled dresses" of the ladies emerging from the private quarters of the Prince of the Peace, while the Queen would scream and rage in her apartments no more than twenty yards distant.

Though one need not accept Godoy's claim that he worked eighteen hours a day in the service of his country (such a reckoning would presumably include his work at night), his domestic policy was generally enlightened and progressive. The majority of his reforms were supported by liberal thinkers, including the writers Moratín and Meléndez Valdez, as well as the greatest painter of the day, Francisco Goya. In political philosophy, Godoy was an eighteenth-century traditionalist who placed great faith in founding educational institutes for the betterment of the people, thus obliquely undermining the Church's predominant role in the field of learning. In 1795, the Royal Medical College was founded in Madrid, and throughout the country schools for handicrafts and technical training were encouraged. The restrictive censorship laws passed by Floridablanca were greatly relaxed, and it was one of Godoy's more justifiable boasts in later life that no one had suffered persecution at his hands.

Unfortunately, in the eyes of the majority of the nation, Godoy remained forever the *choricero*, the "sausage-maker," an allusion to a specialty of his native province. If the King was pitied, Godoy and the Queen were despised and held jointly responsible for every misfortune and setback. On August 18, 1796, the treaty of San Ildefonso was signed between France and Spain, an agreement to lend mutual assistance in the event of war. Two months later, hostilities broke out with England, culminating in a naval defeat off Cape St. Vincent and the temporary severance of communications with the restless overseas colonies. At the same time, General Bonaparte was leading his armies to victory in Italy. Flushed with success, it is doubtful that he gave more than a passing thought to Spain's predicament.

On a more personal level, Godoy found himself accused by María Luisa of *lèse majesté* of the worst sort, namely gross neglect and infidelity due to the intrusion of the youthful Pepita Tudó, who had replaced the aging, toothless Queen in Manuel's affections. Although the affair with Pepita was to last many years and produce two illegitimate children, Godoy decided that his legal wife should be of the royal blood. Having briefly considered marrying Louis XVI's daughter, he finally settled for Charles IV's niece, Teresa de Borbón y Vallabriga, thus officially attaching himself to the reigning family. A few weeks after the wedding, he was back with Pepita, and an indignant Rohde noted that "after he had drawn the dowry of five million reals, Godoy had the effrontery to return immediately to the Tudó, with whom he lived more intimately than ever." To her credit, the discarded Queen seems to have accepted the situation philosophically, and in later years regarded Pepita, Teresa, and the resultant offspring with genuine motherly affection.

The details of Godoy's temporary dismissal as First Minister in 1798 have never been fully explained. Suggestions have been made that it was due largely to the momentary displeasure of the Queen, or to the hostility of Jovellanos, author of the reformist *Informe sobre la ley agraria* (Report on the Agrarian Law), or to the intrigues of the Marquis of Caballero. Whatever the reason, Godoy remained the power behind the throne and continued to enjoy the royal confidence. His successor in office was the anticlerical Urquijo, himself only thirty years old, who kept things in the family by selecting Godoy's sister Antonia, the Marquesa de Branciforte, as his mistress. As Urquijo was considered too "Jansenist" by the Church, he, in turn, was replaced by Pedro Ceballos, a relative of Godoy. Neither was very successful in running the country, and it was not long before the Prince of the Peace was recalled. In the meantime, Bonaparte had become First Consul through a coup d'état; Godoy, on his return to office, no longer would be dealing with an impotent, faceless Directory.

Bonaparte's accession to power was welcomed with a display of official enthusiasm by Charles IV "so as to prove, not only to France, but to the whole of Europe, the pleasure that these events have caused Their Majesties." A year later, he addressed the First Consul as *"Grande y bien amado Amigo,"* a term usually reserved for the nobility. Clearly, the dominant personality in Spain was not the titular head but the Prince of the Peace, as Bonaparte had perceived many years earlier. In his monumental work on Napoleon in Spain, André Fugier observes:

Up to the autumn of 1807, the history of Napoleon's relations with Spain is that of his relations with Godoy. Rarely have such dissimilar politicians been opposed to one another. On the one hand, we have the pliant and profligate favorite, but short-sighted and plainly selfish, with his eyes always turned towards his powerful neighbor whom he distrusts and fears, but who nevertheless would like to gather up some crumbs of the latter's prodigious fortune. [Godoy] is sometimes sulky and even insolent, sometimes flattering and urgent, always busying himself with confused and complicated dealings, always quibbling, evasive, lying, dealing underhand, ready for changing political fortunes. On the other hand, we have the imperious and hurried master who thinks of his ally only when in need of his services, who asks for, claims, demands them, scolds, threatens and finally extorts a cooperation which he always finds sluggish and insufficient, is irritated by the indolent, powerless and ridiculous Bourbons, but as yet does not think of replacing this senile and worn-out line by his own.

Soon these two headstrong figures would clash with one another.

By 1800 Godoy was officially back in power, the same year in which Goya painted his unflattering portrait of the royal family. The arrogant young man to the left in the canvas is Fernando, Prince of the Asturias, successor to the throne, who bitterly resented the favorite's ascendency over his parents to his own detriment. Already his tutor, Juan Escoiquiz, had poisoned the young prince's mind against his mother and Godoy, and this early animosity was soon to turn into venomous hatred. Bonaparte was kept fully informed, and was also *au courant* regarding the royal boudoir, where María Lusia had taken on yet another lover, a South American named Malló. The incident is related of Godoy telling the King in the Queen's presence that Malló was without a penny of his own, "but they say that he is kept by some toothless old woman who robs her husband to enrich her lover." The King smiled innocently, and apparently the Queen bravely dismissed the impudent remark as one of Manuel's little jokes.

In March 1801, with Bonaparte's full connivance, Spain declared war on Portugal. The fighting lasted only a few days, resulting in an easy victory for Spain in the War of the Oranges; the soldiers occupied themselves by cutting orange twigs and capturing enemy cattle. The campaign, led by Godoy himself, had been so brief that no French forces were involved, and once again *el Príncipe de la Paz* justified his exalted title. Recently, Bonaparte had sent his trouble-making brother Lucien to Spain as French ambassador. The latter suggested to Godoy that the Portuguese war indemnity could be put to practical use: "Fifteen million for the government, ten for us.... One has to seize such opportunities, they do not come along every day." Napoleon was determined to impose onerous conditions on the vanquished nation, but the two intriguers innocently pretended that the peace treaty had already been signed before the courier arrived from Paris. A flurry of furious missives had no effect; in one of Godoy's replies Napoleon encountered the phrase, "from one soldier to another," which must have been the cruelest cut of all.

Lucien, in common with the Bonaparte clan, had never approved of his brother's marriage to Josephine, and on his own initiative sought out a suitable replacement. His fellow conspirators in this bizarre scheme were Manuel and María Luisa, who thought that the Infanta Isabel would make the ideal choice. When news of the project reached the First Consul, he exploded: "If I were in a position to marry again, I would not look for a wife in a royal house in ruin." As for Godoy, Bonaparte commented, "I can make use of him, but all I owe him is contempt." More irritations followed; Godoy not only boasted of further feats of valor, but also intimated that Spain might conclude a separate peace treaty with England.

The remaining French troops on Spanish soil—ostensibly allies—were a persistent source of friction. The francophobe population deprived the foreigners of provisions and medical supplies, with frequent altercations and occasional murders. Godoy demanded that no new troops enter and that the remainder leave as soon as possible. An enraged Bonaparte avowed that, had it been another nation, war would have been declared, but as France and Spain enjoyed a special relationship, he would therefore generously overlook their faults. In a darker moment he facetiously asked the Spanish ambassador: "Is is possible that your masters are so tired of reigning that they wish to expose their throne by provoking a war which could have the direst results?" Clearly, the barb was aimed at the *Santa Trinidad* as a whole; Bonaparte was aware that in Godoy he was confronted with an elusive adversary.

On March 25, 1802, the Peace of Amiens hopefully concluded the lengthy wars between France and England. As usual, Spanish interests were ignored and the island of Trinidad was bartered away; when hostilities were resumed, Bonaparte sold the Louisiana Territory to the United States, breaking a solemn promise to Spain that he would not do so. Godoy, newly appointed Generalissimo, was powerless to intervene, knowing that his military strength was as ineffective as the new saber of honor bestowed on him by the King. Spain, in order to remain uninvolved in the new war, was called upon by her irksome ally to pay a considerable subsidy regardless of widespread famine and an outbreak of yellow fever. One day, Godoy received an anonymous gift of a loaf of bread that had been deftly quartered; the threat was unmistakable. Nor was he consoled by the knowledge that Napoleon and Talleyrand were undermining his position by direct communications to the King. Fortunately, his influence over the royal couple was as secure as ever, and in a personal letter, María Luisa assured Manuel that his "memory and fame will endure until the end of the world." (Both monarchs addressed Godoy by his first name and the familiar "*tú*," whereas Napoleon called his brothers by their official titles and the formal "*vous*," at least in correspondence.)

Napoleon, recently proclaimed Emperor, was pragmatic enough to abandon his negative tactics; besides, he was evolving an ambitious plan that would require the full cooperation of the Spanish navy. Accordingly, Godoy found himself back in the imperial favor, even receiving a direct message that began with the cordial salutation "*mon cousin*." This improvement in their relationship was most timely, as Charles IV was suffering from apoplexy, and the *privado* feared that Fernando and his wife, Marie Antoinette of Naples, might succeed to the throne. By chance, a compromising letter in which the Princess confided to her mother that "in case the King died, the Prince of the Peace would be arrested within half an hour" fell into the hands of Napoleon, who obligingly sent a copy of the incriminating document to Godoy. María Lusia detested her daughter-in-law even more than she disliked her own son (the young couple also happened to be first cousins) and in a letter to Manuel she described her as "the spittle of her mother, a venomous viper, an animal filled with gall and poison in place of blood, a half-dead frog and a diabolical snake" bent on encompassing the death of the reigning monarchs. Ironically, it was the Princess herself who died on May 21, 1806, at the age of twenty-three, but such was Godoy's unpopularity in Spain that her premature death was imputed to the *choricero,* poison being the supposed instrument. The fact that her health had been debilitated by tuberculosis and two miscarriages was conveniently ignored, though María Luisa uncharitably hinted that syphilis might have been a contributory factor.

Such a family spectacle was the stuff that Napoleon's dreams were made of. He had already removed Charles IV's brother from the throne of Naples with the minimum of protest; the next step was to relocate the King's daughter ruling over the Kingdom of Etruria in northern Italy. Here, the division of Portugal fitted neatly into Napoleon's ambitious plans, for the Prince Regent was as mentally unbalanced as most of the ruling families in Europe. With his customary generosity (when it came to dividing up other nations' territories), Napoleon offered compensation to the dispossessed monarchs in Portugal, even to the extent of carving out a kingdom for Godoy in the southern part. For the next two years, like some dissolute Sancho Panza, Godoy longed for his ideal realm to which he could retire; that Napoleon had no intention of keeping his vague promise did not cross his mind. The truth was that the naval defeat at Trafalgar in October 1805 had considerably weakened Godoy's position, no matter how much he attempted to minimize the disaster in optimistic dispatches to Napoleon.

Godoy had much on which to ruminate. Now completely overshadowed by Napoleon, his support was taken so much for granted that he was never consulted; once, for a period of six months, there was no French ambassador at the Court of Their Catholic Majesties. Fantastic rumors abounded to the effect that Louis Napoleon was near death and that his widow, Hortense (who was also Napoleon's step-daughter) would marry Fernando, that Lucien would be King of Spain before the year was out, that further territorial divisions were contemplated. When Godoy complained that only the King received any official correspondence, he was informed that the French Emperor regarded him as part of an indissoluble Trinity, thus eliminating the need for individual letters. Godoy decided to take matters into his own hands, and on October 5, 1806, he issued an extraordinary proclamation calling the nation to arms but without specifying the identity of the enemy. The news of the Prussian defeat at Jena rendered any speculation purely theoretical as Godoy hastened to assure Napoleon that Portugal was the country he had in mind. In his *Memorias,* with retrospective courage, he maintained that the mobilization was directed against France—probably true, but as so often in his foreign policies, totally ineffective and irrelevant.

While the health of Charles IV continued to fluctuate alarmingly, the latest rumors had it that Fernando's next wife would either be a niece of Murat's or Lucien's daughter Charlotte. Napoleon's disdain for the Bourbon *ménage* was tempered by diplomatic cynicism; the time was not yet ripe for open intervention, and even as the King was being bled to reduce a high fever, the Emperor sought to reassure the Spanish ambassador with honeyed words:

> If I thought of dethroning Charles IV, what would my other allies say about me, and what confidence would they have in an alliance with me in the future? ... I am the friend of Spain out of a sense of duty and sentiment, it is in my own interest and policy. No one respects more than I the personal character of Charles IV, no one knows or esteems more highly the qualities and virtues of the Castillian people; we saw them at Trafalgar, without having to search further. Let us not talk about war. ... Also write to your friend, the Prince of the Peace. His position, if he can keep it, is such that History will be able to dedicate a fine page to him for having protected his country from revolutions and wars which everywhere have afflicted nations ... [but] his fall is certain if he changes his policy.

To give Spain an opportunity to prove her friendship to France, Napoleon requested that 14,000 troops be sent to garrison cities in northern Germany; Godoy complied immediately. For added protection, however, he increased his own bodyguard and placed himself in charge of palace security.

In early 1807 Charles IV heaped further titles on his favorite, including that of Grand Admiral, despite the fact that Manuel was often seasick. Once, on hearing that Napoleon had suffered the loss of a battle horse, the King hastened to send a pair of fine stallions; Godoy, not to be outdone, matched the royal gift. He was acutely aware that this was no more than a façade while events vital to Spain's future were gathering momentum. There was no hint of what had transpired at Napoleon's meeting with

Czar Alexander I at Tilsit (small wonder, as the two Emperors had informally discussed momentous changes that were to take place in Spain); and when in July Portugal was given an unacceptable ultimatum to close its ports to the English, Godoy could only speculate as to what Napoleon had in mind. The dispatch of French units across the Spanish border, supposedly in transit to quell the insubordinate Portuguese, was sanctioned by the Treaty of Fontainebleau (October 29), signed nearly two weeks *ex post facto*. Again, Godoy was the spectator rather than the participant; had he been aware of Fernando's recent clandestine overtures to Napoleon, many uncertainties would have been accounted for.

More and more, the focus of opposition to the royal favorite was centering in the person of the Infante, now twenty-three years old. When Napoleon heard that Fernando had lost his wife, his immediate reaction was, "We will have to think about replacing her"—hence the rumors of a French betrothal. The French ambassador to Madrid was anxious to suggest the name of Marie-Stéphanie Tascher de la Pagerie, both his and Josephine's cousin, and generally considered an excellent choice. Napoleon persuaded the young Prince to put his secret request for the hand of a French princess in writing, it being tacitly understood that he would soon be placed on his father's throne. The scheme was discovered, and in a dramatic confrontation with his enraged parents, Fernando tearfully confessed to all, including a plot to have his mother murdered. The Infante was placed under guard in his room at the Escorial palace, certain that he would be executed in much the same way Philip II had supposedly removed his son Don Carlos in 1568.

But Fernando was to be saved in the most unexpected manner possible, thanks to the intervention of Godoy, who was well aware of the Prince's popularity among the people and also of the hatred directed against himself. In all probability he thought that Fernando had debased himself enough and that his collusion with the French required no further proof. Godoy was conscious of the pressure exerted by Napoleon, who instructed his ambassador not to mince matters with Charles IV:

> Tell him that from this moment I am taking the Prince of the Asturias [Fernando] under my protection. If he is touched—however little—or if my ambassador is insulted, or if the mobilized army does not leave immediately for Portugal according to our agreement, I shall declare war on Spain, and I shall place myself at the head of my army to invade it.

At the Prince's subsequent trial, which began on January 25, 1808, Napoleon's role in the affair was not mentioned and the case against Fernando collapsed. Godoy was loathed more than ever for having been involved in the matter, even though he had saved the Prince's life and was one of the few to recognize the true nature of the threat to Spain. As for Marie-Stéphanie, she married the Prince of Arenberg on February 1, no doubt glad to have escaped so easily.

There was now no halting the dénouement. The Portuguese royal family had already made good their flight to Brazil, and Godoy suggested that a similar strategy—or at least the transfer of the royal court to southern Spain—might become necessary in the future. Confronted with growing French military pressure (the fortresses of Montjuich and Pamplona had already been occupied by Spain's "allies"), he raised the possibility of a government in exile. The most that Charles IV would agree to was the removal of the Court to the royal palace at Aranjuez, a short distance to the south of the capital.

Godoy now became thoroughly alarmed. For the first time, the King wavered in his support; and with the approach of the French army under Murat—Napoleon's brother-in-law, renowned for his bold exploits—the growing assembly of opportunists surrounding Fernando gained confidence. On Thursday, March 17, the gardens of the royal residence were filled with a crowd of *Madrileños* and unruly soldiers, who towards evening became an infuriated mob bent on seizing the detested favorite. Godoy's house was ransacked, though his wife was given safe conduct through the screaming rabble. The intended quarry was nowhere to be found, having hidden under a pile of carpets in the attic. Thirty-six hours later, suffering from intense thirst, he ventured out, only to be arrested by a guard. Upon being recognized by other soldiers, he was subjected to blows and knife wounds, surely the preliminary to being lynched by the mob. At this critical juncture, Fate chose to repeat itself, merely reversing the earlier roles. Fernando was summoned in haste, and sensing that he would soon be declared the new sovereign, magnanimously saved Godoy's life by handing him over to the proper authorities. Soon afterwards, a frightened Charles IV abdicated in favor of the son who had conspired against his parents. Their sole request was that Manuel's life be spared.

In theory, the Aranjuez palace revolution should have settled everything: the Spanish nation was rid of the *privado* and had received the King it desired, and Napoleon now had a compliant tool on the throne. But the French Emperor's appetite had been whetted by this fortuitous turn of events, and perhaps—with a little encouragement from Murat and the French army—he might even be able to place his brother Joseph on the Spanish throne. Fernando was at a loss to understand why the French still withheld official recognition, but allowed himself to be persuaded that a face-to-face meeting with Napoleon would soon settle matters to his advantage.

Despite several warnings as to the French stratagem, Fernando left Madrid towards the north, only to discover repeatedly that his rendezvous with the Emperor remained at a tantalizing distance. Finally, he crossed the Rubicon—or, rather, the small Bidassoa river that marked the border—and arrived at Bayonne on the French side. To his chagrin, he discovered that Napoleon had assembled an intimate reunion which not only included the Spanish royal family but also a somewhat battered Godoy, who had been spirited out of the country under French guard. The purpose of this gathering *en famille* soon became clear: Napoleon announced that the Bourbons had ceased to rule in Spain and that his own brother Joseph had graciously agreed (with a little prodding, he might have added) to ascend the throne. Fernando threw a lachrymose tantrum in vain; upon receiving news of the grave disturbances in Madrid on May 2 and 3—the *Dos* and *Tres de Mayo* depicted by Goya—Napoleon insisted on the prompt legalization of his "solution," and Charles IV once again was forced to abdicate, this time in favor of Joseph. For Godoy, this was the encounter with Napoleon he had so long anticipated, but hardly under the circumstances he had envisaged. Napoleon's behavior was correct, but distant; he preferred to look towards the future, and now the *privado* was a pathetic figure from the past.

Godoy was forty-two years old and had reached exactly the halfway point of his life. His career was ended, and the remaining years would be spent in unhappy exile without once returning to his native land. In Larra's pithy statement, "Don Manuel Godoy was condemned to become a spectator of the fallen Prince of the Peace." The elderly Charles and María Luisa, togther with Pepita Tudó, Manuel and their children, first established their residence in the Château de Compiègne, but because of the dampness and the poor hunting, they soon headed south to Marseilles where they remained four years, living in genteel poverty. In July 1812 the whole family moved to Rome, where Godoy occasionally dressed up in the splendid uniforms of his past glory for the benefit of visitors.

Two years later, Fernando "the Desired," who had been Talleyrand's unwilling guest at the latter's Château de Valençay, returned to Spain as King. The intervening years and distance had not diminished his hatred for his mother and Godoy; agents were sent to spy upon the privacy of the exiled family, and rivalries and dissensions were fomented. The passing years had taken their toll, and the health of the royal couple slowly declined. Finally, in January 1819 María Luisa breathed her last, watched over by the ever-faithful Manuel, who himself very nearly died shortly afterwards. Seventeen days later, Charles IV followed his wife to the grave.

Godoy's remaining thirty-two years were spent in frustration and lonely reminiscence. Deprived of his titles, entirely dependent on charity and a negligible income, the Prince of the Peace soon became an almost forgotten figure. Upon the death of the wife who had refused to follow him into exile, he finally married Pepita, only to see her desert him in later years, leaving him alone in Paris. Pepita had traveled to Spain to plead Manuel's cause, and her failure to return was a bitter blow. Even the death of Fernando in 1833 after a tyrannical reign did little to improve his precarious situation. In an effort to raise much-needed funds, as well as refurbish his tarnished political reputation, he wrote the *Memorias* in 1836-37. Despite many inaccuracies, due in part to lack of accessible material, they are written with verve and perspicacity, each page revealing the generous attitude of the author.

Toward the end of his long life, Godoy was visited in his modest apartment in Paris by the Spanish essayist Mesonero Romanos, who has left us a sympathetic portrayal of a gentle old man playing innocent games with the local children in the gardens of the Palais Royal. Few suspected that "Monsieur Manuel" at one time had shared the political stage with the great Emperor Napoleon himself; even his own daughter, who lived nearby, preferred to ignore him. The last few years were spent in a humiliating correspondence with the government in Madrid. Finally, on May 31, 1847, Queen Isabel II restored his rank and property, but it was now much too late for the aged exile to travel to Spain and claim his due. The end came on October 4, 1851, one year before Napoleon's nephew was acclaimed Emperor of the French; Godoy's burial in the Père Lachaise cemetery passed almost unnoticed. Stirring events were afoot in Paris, the glories of the Napoleonic Empire were to be revived—of what concern was the death of an old man when the future seemed to hold so much promise?

Francisco Goya

Seneca, the Roman statesman and philosopher born in Córdoba in southern Spain, and one of the most perceptive writers of the first century A.D. once observed:

> We are mad, not only individually, but nationally. We check manslaughter and isolated murders; but what of war and the much vaunted crime of slaughtering whole peoples?

Seventeen centuries later his words would assume prophetic force during the internecine war provoked by the Napoleonic invasion of Spain in 1808 and again during the destructive tragedy of the Civil War of 1936-39. Seneca knew his people well; but no Spaniard has portrayed the emotions and character of his fellow citizens with such graphic power and penetration as Francisco Goya, court painter and chronicler of man's darkest re-

cesses. It is said that his servant once asked him why he
recorded the barbarities that men committed. Goya's
reply was: "To tell men forever that they should not
be barbarians."

Francisco Goya y Lucientes was born in a small
Aragonese village near Saragossa in 1746. His apprenticeship was served under his father, a local gilder, and various artists painting in the prevalent baroque style. A
pilgrimage to study in Italy was still considered a *sine
qua non,* though ironically Goya's visit must almost have
coincided with Winckelmann's publication in 1764 of his
masterpiece reassessing Greek art, which provided the
underpinning for the classical revival. Of greater immediacy were the Esquilache riots in Madrid which Goya
witnessed in March 1766. Directed against foreign styles
of dress and the prevalence of Italian ministers at the
Court, the riots were an affirmation of Spanish traditions.
Seeing Madrid for the first time, the provincial youth
must have been both bewildered and exhilarated by the
political and artistic crosscurrents that were to prevail in
the capital during the last third of the eighteenth century.

Goya's early paintings are not merely conventional;
they reveal a somewhat cynical versatility to adapt to
whatever style a patron, whether lay or ecclesiastical,
might require. Thus the first years are marked by an
eclectic conformity, offering uninspired examples of
rococo church interiors as well as themes handled in the
classical manner. This ability to work simultaneously on
conflicting subjects in a wide range of styles was to remain
characteristic of Goya throughout his life. At this period
he appears to have been indifferent to political and social
questions of the day, directing his energies to becoming an
official court painter. A useful step toward fulfilling this
aim was his marriage in 1773 to Josefa Bayeu, the sister
of one of the leading artists of the neo-classical school of

Mengs. A stern, humorless man, Francisco Bayeu never-theless taught his temperamental brother-in-law new techniques and, regardless of many personal frictions, was to further Goya's career.

The first positive results were the pastoral scenes de-picted in some of the early cartoons that Goya painted for the royal tapestries. Typically Spanish were the swag-gering figures of the *majos* and *majas,* elegantly dressed ruffians whose unrestricted lifestyle was the envy of poor and aristocrat alike. Though more charming than original, the cartoons for the first time give a hint of what lay ahead; in Antonina Vallentin's words, "the Goya of the cartoons was a little like a great poet who first sketches, in prose that is a little banal, the elements of future poems that will be immortal." The real breakthrough in his career, however, was the commission to paint the portrait of Count Floridablanca, the First Minister to Charles III. Like Goya, the Count was of humble origins, a liberal and an opponent of obscurantism; the main difference was that at the age of thirty-seven, Goya had still failed to make a reputation, whereas Floridablanca—as his official portrait amply shows—entertained no doubt as to his exalted position. The First Minister dominates the canvas, surrounded by the insignia and paraphernalia of his office; a haughty face stares fixedly towards the viewer, completely ignoring his timid secretary in the background and the deferential presence of the artist who is holding a canvas up to him. The painting is no masterpiece—in fact, a neo-classical vapidity—but it heralds Goya's rapid ascent and recognition as a portraitist. With fame came wealth and a certain degree of artistic independence which, in turn, led to new means of artistic expression.

Goya now had acquired entrée both to aristocratic society as well as to the world of letters. Though acutely aware of their lineage and social standing, many of Spain's noblest families were imbued with a democratic spirit that cheerfully embraced the company of *majos,* bullfighters, writers, and artists. Goya, now in his early forties, embarked on a series of individual and family portraits, including those of the wealthy Osuna family and the Infante Don Luis, the King's brother. In the latter group-portrait, the Infante's delightful two-year-old daughter, María Teresa, is entranced by the artist sitting at his easel; seventeen years later Goya portrayed her as the wife of Manuel Godoy, revealing all the pent-up suffering of a loveless marriage. No such hint of future tragedy is apparent in these early works, but Goya's propensity for unequal quality, often a reflection of his personal attitude toward his sitter soon became well-known and the subject of much comment. The portrait of Charles III in hunting dress shows great affection and understanding for his royal patron, whereas Count Cabarrus, the father of Madame Tallien, is unimaginatively depicted in a strained pose.

On September 21, 1789, began three days of official celebrations to fête the accession of Charles IV and María Luisa as the new sovereigns of Spain; the Bastille was still a world away. Though Goya was irritated by his obligations to complete work on the royal tapestries, commissions from the wealthy, as well as from actors and personal friends, continued to pour in. During this outwardly complacent phase of his life, an inner turmoil was gathering force within the artist that paralleled much of the intellectual anguish of progressive politicians and writers such as Goya's friend, Jovellanos. While continuing in many instances to rely on traditional methods, Goya increasingly came to favor shorter and heavier brush strokes, even using rags and sponges to apply the paint, working as quickly as possible to seize the first impression and transfer it to canvas. The backgrounds become darker, devoid of unnecessary detail; the emphasis is placed on revealing the individual character of his sitter or the social impact of the group. The joint influence of Rembrandt and Velásquez becomes increasingly noticeable in the use of chiaroscuro for greater psychological effect.

In 1792, the same fateful year that Manuel Godoy took over the reins of government from Floridablanca, Goya was stricken with a severe malady during a visit to Andalucia. For a time it was feared that he would lose his eyesight, perhaps even his life. The resultant partial paralysis and deafness recreated the artist and endowed him with a powerful inner vision. Spain, soon to be at war with revolutionary France, was losing its complacency, and the squalid affair rumored between the Queen and Godoy was to shake the nation's traditional faith in its leaders. Goya saw society at all levels as hiding behind a mask to conceal its debased nature: it mattered little whether his subjects were officials of the Inquisition or peasants celebrating the end of the carnival season. All are insane, as is every crowd that gathers, whether to watch a procession of flagellants, a bullfight, or the inmates of the madhouse; soon spectators and victims are united in a collective delirium. The series of paintings Goya termed "popular diversions" was his introspective foray into the world of mass hysteria, superstition, and ignorance, a theme to which he would return with even greater force.

Some time during 1795 he became acquainted with the Duke and Duchess of Alba. The latter's wealth matched, if not exceeded, that of the royal family, and the mutual hostility between the Queen and the Duchess served as a constant topic of scandal that helped relegate the ominous events in Paris into the background. After the death of the Duke in 1796, Goya spent several months

at the Alba estate in Sanlúcar near Cádiz comforting the
widow, who had been banished from Madrid by a vengeful María Luisa. The two full-length portraits of the
strong-willed Duchess, though brilliant technically, are
somewhat stiff and lacking in vivacity. The sketches Goya
made in his notebook during this period are far more
spontaneous and characteristic of the Duchess, who is
captured in all her *maja* sprightliness with a naturalness
that foreshadows the later series of etchings on less
happy subjects. Goya was now over fifty, a gruff, mus-
cular, still unsophisticated provincial; the Duchess, nearly
twenty years younger, yearned for more dashing company. The affair was over, and the saddened artist returned to Madrid and his gloomy innermost thoughts.

As so often in his life, Goya now began work on two
entirely dissimilar projects. In 1798 he was commissioned
to decorate the interior of the new church of San Antonio
de la Florida with scenes depicting a miracle performed
by the saint. Not only the central figures, but especially
the characters in the jostling crowd, show a liveliness and
uninhibited wonder that is an artistic miracle in itself.
Several years after his death in France, Goya's body was
brought back to Madrid and buried before the altar of
the church he had transformed into new life, much as
San Antonio had restored the dead man. His epitaph
might well be that of Sir Christopher Wren in St. Paul's
Cathedral: *"Si monumentum requiris, circumspice."*

At about the same time, Goya began a series of
etchings that bore the general title of *Caprichos,* supposedly an innocent series of whimsical etchings designed
to hold a mirror up to society. Such an ingenuous defense
deceived no one, least of all his contemporaries. The
eighty *Caprichos* form a sequence of biting satire, underlined by the artist's mordant comments that accompany

146

each scene. Grotesque and hallucinatory, they are a devastating summation of Spain's social and political sicknesses. Though Godoy had somewhat reluctantly plunged his country into war with France, he had managed to emerge with the fanciful title of Prince of the Peace. He had once boasted that his name signified "*godo soy*" and that therefore his ancestry stretched back to the Goths; Goya has portrayed a donkey diligently studying his genealogy in like fashion. Nor did the Duchess of Alba escape unscathed for her flippant dismissal of the artist. But such personal allusions are incidental to the main theme of the *Caprichos,* which is the terrifying specter of madness in all its forms. In one etching, a man—perhaps Goya himself—is slumped across a table in despair as a hideous cacophony assails him from a swarm of nocturnal creatures. The caption below—a commentary by the artist— reads "The sleep of reason produces monsters." The eighteenth century, which had prided itself as the Age of Enlightenment, was dead, and an era of irrational horrors, so tellingly delineated in the *Caprichos,* was about to begin.

Whatever his personal feelings might have been, in his public conduct Goya demonstrated a characteristic ambivalence of behavior. Apparently succumbing to the flattering attentions of Godoy—who had even learned the rudiments of sign language in order to converse with the deaf painter—Goya painted the royal favorite's wife and, soon afterwards, the Prince of the Peace himself bedecked in his military finery. Godoy's wife, the King's niece and now the Countess of Chinchón, has lost all traces of the childlike innocence that Goya had captured seventeen years previously; in a psychological materpiece, Goya has portrayed her inner despair as she bears the child of her callous husband. A dissolute Godoy is shown in a most unmilitary pose, his bulky frame reclining in an ornamental chair against an unconvincing setting. Goya may be faulted with ambiguous loyalties throughout his life; but his inner artistic voice spoke with forthright honesty. Nowhere is this more apparent than in his devastating portrait of the Family of Charles IV, painted in 1800. Surely no artist has ever depicted collective decadence for posterity with a sharper twist of the brush. Goya, now well into his fifties, had finally acquired the full confidence of his mature genius.

His appointment as First Painter to the King in 1799 failed to assuage his growing misanthropy and withdrawal into an inner world. Soon his friend Jovellanos would be incarcerated on the flimsiest of charges, and in 1802 the Duchess of Alba died mysteriously, just forty years old. At the height of his artistic powers and fame, Goya in effect entered into semiretirement. There are no more royal portraits, and the paintings of this barren period are difficult to date with any accuracy because they vary in technique and inspiration. It was only the Napoleonic invasion and resultant national crisis of 1808 that re-awakened the dormant genius of Goya at the age of sixty-two. To his personal agonized vision was now added the national anguish of war and widespread destruction.

The predicament in which Goya found himself was typical of many Spanish liberals. Though he had welcomed the abdication of Charles IV and María Luisa, and been elated at the fall of Godoy (in whose possession both portraits of the famous *Maja* were found), the needless slaughter and subsequent reprisals following the popular uprising of the *Dos de Mayo* had transformed initial enthusiasm for the enlightened ideas of the French into deep revulsion. There is little basis to the story that Goya made detailed studies of the fallen victims, but there can be no doubt that the savagery of those hours deeply etched itself into his mind. Six years later, when he painted his two immortal canvases, the details of those terrible events had lost none of their force.

After the unexpected defeat of the French at Bailén and the heroic resistance of besieged Saragossa under José Palafox, Goya returned to his native province and visited the city. Appalled by the destruction during the war's early stages, Goya was moved by the heroism of both the Spanish military and common citizens. His etching of Agustina Zaragoza firing the cannon following the death of its crew acquires symbolic power; the individual assumes national grandeur. In Lovett's words, "She is Saragossa and Spain all in one, the symbol of Spanish resistance to Napoleon."

Two concurrent events were to have a profound effect on Goya's initial attitude. The first was Napoleon's personal direction of the war and the firmer establishment of his brother Joseph on the vacant Spanish throne. Joseph, contrary to much Spanish opinion, was an enlightened liberal, genuinely anxious to introduce reforms such as the abolition of the Inquisition and feudal rights. His ambitious plans for the improvement of Madrid, as well as his generous support of the arts, made this affable monarch truly popular among those few who became accquainted with him. Though Goya never painted a formal portrait of *el rey intruso,* he did copy a likeness of Joseph from a print and display it prominently in his "Allegory of the City of Madrid." In future years this painting was to undergo several changes that reflected the vicissitudes of war; later in the nineteenth century the successive alterations painted over Joseph's portrait were removed and replaced by a scroll bearing the inscription *Dos de Mayo.* More important, Goya painted several French dignitaries during the occupation of Madrid, including General Nicholas Guye and several

Spanish *afrancesados*. In his capacity as Court Painter, Goya was given the task of helping to select fifty Spanish works that were to grace the *Musée Napoléon* in Paris; the paintings chosen were certainly not the best available, and in any case did not leave the country. But Goya's association with the hated invader, and his award of the Order of Spain (dubbed the "eggplant" by the populace), were enough to cast grave doubt on his patriotism, even though he later protested that he never wore his honor.

The second event was a tragic outgrowth of the first. Napoleon's defeat of several Spanish regular armies had crystallized resistance into a spontaneous guerrilla movement that harried the occupation forces. The resultant cruelties practiced by both sides—often of a sadistic nature involving willful mutilation of corpses—thoroughly changed the whole nature of the war. Goya was filled with revulsion at the wanton slaughter and human debasement, and hastened to depict the pillage and destruction in enduring form. The suppressed forces first envisaged in the *Caprichos* now stalked the land, unchecked and run amok. The etchings of the *Desastres de la Guerra* (Disasters of War), based on preliminary sketches made during his visit to Saragossa, portray the horror of total war shorn of any lingering false romanticism; the scenes of rape and other atrocities committed on and by civilians is an eloquent indictment of all wars for all time.

The *Desastres* consist of a series of eighty-two etchings with three additional ones depicting prisoners in chains. Probably Goya thought of publishing them during the liberal hiatus between 1820-23, but for some reason they were restricted to a circle of intimates during the artist's lifetime. One of these, Ceán Bermúdez, suggested the comprehensive title: *Fatales consecuencias de la sangrienta guerra en España con Buonaparte, y otros caprichos enfáticos en 87 estampas* (The Fatal Consequences of the Bloody War in Spain against Buonaparte, and Other Forcible Caprichos in 87 Plates), but the Spanish Academy later wisely chose the incisive heading under which the war scenes are known today.

Still uncertain is the intended order of the etchings. There is no narrative as such, but a general sequence suggests itself. The first group depicts primitive violence on both sides, as soldiers and civilians indulge in a harrowing series of vicious attacks, using knives, axes, stakes, and whatever weapons come to hand; even women holding their children derive a twisted gratification with sexual overtones as they impale French soldiers with goads ("Y son fieras"—"And they are wild beasts" is Goya's trenchant title under the sketch). In rapid succession, further diabolic horrors are portrayed: dismemberment, mass burials, famine, tortures, and hangings ("¿Qué hay que hacer más?"—"What more can be done?" and "¡Gran hazaña! ¡Con muertos!"—"Great prowess! With dead men!" are two of the most powerful etchings of this section). With one prodigious artistic leap, Goya has repudiated the chivalrous conventions of eighteenth-century combat as no longer applicable to show warfare as it is—bestial, unreasoned, and demeaning. It is all uncomfortably modern as we look at the war crimes of our own century.

The second group of etchings becomes increasingly symbolic as the grotesque and ironic elements come to predominate. Less realistic, the figures acquire a universality and timelessness as the details—such as the soldiers' uniforms—are blurred in favor of a sweeping indictment of all violence. Significantly, the sharp black and white gives way to shadings of grey; rather than apportion guilt to one side or the other simply on nationalistic grounds, Goya perceived that the true crime was war itself. In "Sanos y enfermos" ("The sound and the sick") we can barely distinguish between the two as war reduces its victims to the same condition. There are no conventional military scenes in the *Desastres*. Goya devotes the entire series to the sufferings of civilians which he witnessed —"*Yo lo vi*" ("I saw it"), he emphasizes. Goya's anguish in the face of such inhuman (or perhaps all too human) destruction was of an inner nature—in fact the *Desastres* were not made public until 1863, well after the artist's death. Though the two men never met, the etchings are Goya's bitter denunciation of the misery brought by Napoleon to Spain. To Napoleon, war was still an adventure; to Goya, it was barbaric.

During the conflict he remained mostly in Madrid, painting friends and members of his family as well as the occasional passing military figure. On one of his few excursions from the capital, he sketched the Duke of Wellington in Alba de Tormes immediately following the battle of Arápiles (Salamanca) in 1812, a sitting at which blows are said to have been nearly exchanged between general and artist. A later equestrian painting of Wellington is unimpressive, and even the famous portrait representing him in ceremonial uniform is lacking in artistic penetration. The same cannot be said of the full-length painting of Fernando VII on his return from French exile. The barely contained reservoir of the new sovereign's hatred and malevolence is shown in every brush stroke; it is a compendium of the evil that was soon to be unleashed against those very liberals and patriots who had freed Spain from the hated French.

The reactionary rule of Fernando VII inaugurated a period of reprisals, especially directed against those who had served under Joseph. Fortunately, Goya could point to the portraits of Wellington; and even before Fernando's return he had offered to paint the patriotic events of the *Dos* and *Tres de Mayo*. These masterpieces, seething with emotion and elemental passion, unforgettably capture the heroic spirit of the masses. The dominant outstretched figure in the latter canvas is symbolic of the resistance of the entire Spanish people, defiant yet dignified at the moment of death. Nevertheless, Goya was called before the Tribunal of Rehabilitations to defend himself; but largely thanks to the intervention of José Palafox, the hero of Saragossa, he was acquitted. Was Goya in fact an *afrancesado* or, in today's terminology, a collaborator? Given the peculiar conditions and political crosscurrents that form the background of the war, no definite assessment can be made. Lovett concludes:

> Perhaps if Goya had been a lesser genius his reputation as a patriot would have come out more tarnished, perhaps not. The painter must be considered a borderline case in the history of collaboration in the Napoleonic war. His place is somewhere in that nebulous area stretching from passive collaboration through noninvolvement to the edges of patriotism.

Perhaps his true allegiance was to art alone.

Goya, a widower since 1812, again withdrew into his private world of fantasy so cruelly interrupted by the war. In February 1819 he bought a house, soon to become known as *La quinta del sordo* (the house of the deaf man), on the outskirts of Madrid. The inner walls he soon transformed into a projection of his own innermost phantasmagoria. These "black paintings" depict the darkest recesses of human follies, a morbid dream-world that embraces witches, devil-goats, demented pilgrims, and flailing peasants, all intertwined in a series of horrendous visions. These are the shadows of superstition and blind bestiality, an anguished cry that goes unheeded. In a parallel series of etchings, the nightmarish *Disparates* (Follies), human endeavors are shown as mutual deceptions; life is fragile at best, with stupidity, tragedy, and farce all interwoven. Though apparently alluding to now-forgotten contemporary events and personalities, the *Disparates* proclaim man as a beast who has yet to earn the right to call himself human.

The liberal uprising of General Riego in 1820 offered hope that representative government might establish itself in Spain, but the intervention of a French army three years later, at Chateaubriand's instigation—incredibly welcomed on this occasion as liberators—restored Fernando's absolutism. For a brief period in danger of his life, Goya reluctantly at the age of seventy-nine made the arduous journey into self-imposed exile. Though he returned briefly to Madrid and was even welcomed by the King, his work in his native land was finished. Once more the vigorous Aragonese, now an octogenarian, crossed the Pyrenees to pass the remaining months of his life in Bordeaux. Active and alert to the end, he died of a paralytic stroke in April 1828.

Such a multifaceted career eludes a neat judgment. The springs of artistic creativity still remain largely a mystery, and in the case of Goya, a difficult task is made almost impossible. Both in technique and vision, he is the first of the moderns. But Goya goes much further: his anguished patriotism bursts all provincial bonds and directs itself to the theme of all human suffering. This sense of despair is well summarized by Richard Schickel:

> It is a feeling so profound as to preclude all faith in political, social or economic progress, and ordained to regard all temporal leaders, theories and organizations, especially governments, as irrelevant at best and comically tragic (or tragically comic) at worst.

True enough, but fortunately Goya has left us with a glimmer of hope. The *Desastres de la Guerra,* that chronicle of hate and horror, ends on a surprisingly optimistic note as Truth and Reason are reborn in a burst of radiant light. Though dimly perceived at the time, human struggle and sacrifice may not be altogether without purpose. As in his own life, Goya is telling us that adversity is a challenge to be overcome, and that perhaps is the answer to it all.

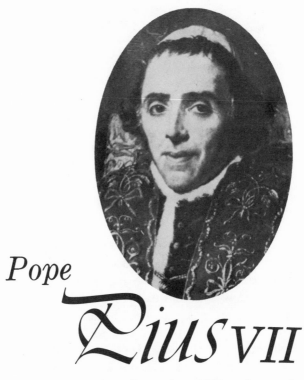

Pope Pius VII

On a wintry day in late December 1812, a battered carriage sped across eastern France towards Paris. The two occupants, the Emperor Napoleon and his Grand Ecuyer, General de Caulaincourt, were immersed in a deep discussion that ranged widely, from the recent disaster in Russia to general philosophizing and personalities. Suddenly, the conversation turned to an unresolved matter that would demand the Emperor's early attention: Pope Pius VII had been arrested three years previously and was now being held prisoner in Fontainebleau. Quite unexpectedly, the elderly pontiff had proved himself firm and determined beneath his gracious manner, revealing unpredicted flashes of temper that contrasted sharply with his usual mildness. Napoleon was frankly puzzled; he thought he had settled his problems with the Church long ago, and here was a stubborn Pope who failed to understand what he, the Emperor, had done for religion since his accession to power. Turning to his companion, he voiced his complaint:

> Not even the most timid consciences, if their owners wished to be fair-minded, could find anything more than a political difference in my disputes with the Pope. The Church has me to thank for the re-establishment of the True Faith in France—perhaps for its survival in Europe —and I am surely as good a Catholic as Charles V was, who also carried off a Pope without becoming a heretic in consequence.

To Napoleon, the relationship between Church and State (i.e., himself) was clearly delineated: "The clergy must be restricted to reconciling us with heaven—to consoling our women and us, when we grow old—and must surrender to us the power of this world: *Roi dans le temple, sujet à la porte.*" Couldn't the Pope grasp this basic concept? As it was, with the *Grande Armée* in disarray and rebellious talk increasingly common, it was a distinct irritation to have to confront his recalcitrant prisoner yet again over such a simple matter. The truth, of course, was far more complex, and the origins of the conflict dated from the very first days of the Revolution, long before either Napoleon or Pope Pius VII had risen to their elevated positions. Accordingly, we must briefly return to the last days of the *ancien régime*.

On May 4, 1789, the spectators at Versailles were awed by the splendid procession to celebrate the convocation of the States-General. At the formal opening there were no dissidents, at least not visibly. Each representative, as he held his lighted candle before him, assumed his designated position, as first the lower clergy, then the numerous delegates of the Third Estate, followed by the nobility and the ecclesiastical hierarchy, all wended their dignified way to attend the High Mass about to be celebrated by the Archbishop of Paris. Bringing up the rear, directly behind the Consecrated Host, walked King Louis XVI, dressed in his most magnificent vestments and symbolizing the historic union between Crown and the Gallican Church. The *ancien régime* was alive, but not very well; had its financial health been better, there would have been no need to convene this bothersome assembly.

The Revolution at the outset was neither irreligious nor anti-Catholic. Many of the rural clergy and the more progressive among the bishops welcomed the opportunity to enact reforms and, in keeping with traditional French practice, turned to the King rather than the Pope for guidance in church matters. Quite unintentionally, it was the insistence of the lower clergy to vote as individual representatives rather than by orders as in the past— thereby giving the Third Estate an assured majority— that opened up the floodgates which would require a Napoleon to close. The early moderation soon gave way to revolutionary forces over which little or no control could be exercised and which, at one point, nearly led to the extinction of the Church in France.

One of the more prominent candle-bearers was the newly appointed Bishop of Autun, better known to history as Charles Maurice de Talleyrand. Widely respected as a progressive if not as a dedicated churchman, in the growing delirium that was possessing the National Assembly he proposed that church property should be taken over by the state to avert national bankruptcy. Gripped by revolutionary momentum and a sense of *mea culpa,* some of the clergy went further and voted for the abolition of tithes and the dissolution of religious orders, agreeing to the restructuring and reduction of the dioceses to conform to the new civil *départements.* In the future, the bishops were to be elected by popular vote which included Protestants and Jews, but by now it was clear to many of the First Estate that the changes embodied in the *Constitution Civile du Clergé* had overstepped the bounds of acceptable reform. Significantly, the Assembly had encroached on canon law; a state religion was one thing, but a Church subject to the State was quite another. Moreover, despite their Gallicanism, the more conservative clerics were turning to the Pope for guidance as the situation worsened.

The first crisis, marking a sharp divergence between the lay revolutionary forces and the Church, came on November 27, 1790; all bishops and priests were given eight days in which to take an oath to the new national Constitution. Those who refused would be deprived of their church benefice, but their dilemma became infinitely more acute when the King was coerced into signing the measure even in the face of the Pope's strong denunciation. Only four bishops—one of whom was Talleyrand—took the oath, but the hostile attitude of the Constituent Assembly precipitated an ecclesiastical emigration that left many bishoprics vacant. These were filled by the open elections as prescribed by the Constitution; henceforth the Church was divided into the *clergé réfractaire*—those who refused to submit—and the *clergé constitutionel*. The consecration of the newly elected bishops was performed by Talleyrand, who was promptly excommunicated. The Pope had already lost Avignon and Venaissin, the two remaining papal territories in France, but his action in calling upon the crowned heads of Europe to restore the *status quo ante* by invasion contributed in part to the slaughter of priests and to the later execution of the King.

The Church now found itself in grave danger, both from within and without. The cleavage between the two contending groups rapidly assumed political implications, the *clergé réfractaire* generally considered to be inimical to the Revolution. The September 1792 massacres killed over two hundred priests of both factions, and the subsequent Terror resulted in further decimations. Hébert's vicious tracts and Fouché's insistence on the clergy getting married within a month produced numerous resignations that left most congregations without a priest to officiate at Mass.

By 1795 the Revolution had spent much of its anticlerical fury, and the next year Pope Pius VI in a pastoral letter exhorted the surviving clergy to submit to the laws of the land. Though occasional persecutions still occurred, the Directory was anxious for some compromise that would ensure peace; but their republican fanaticism rendered a true reconciliation impossible, and the opportunity was lost.

Pius VI had been Pope since 1775, and was already seventy-nine years old when General Bonaparte, a mere twenty-seven, first invaded northern Italy. The elderly head of the Church was as much concerned with the administration of the Papal States as with spiritual matters, a Renaissance prince more familiar with nepotism than the alleviation of poverty in his territories. As a secular authority, he sought protection from fellow conservative rulers. Unfortunately, the chief of these, Emperor Joseph II of Austria, had become infected with the progressive ideas of the Enlightenment and had anticipated many of the reforms taking place in France. The Austrian armies had difficulty enough defending themselves against the unorthodox thrusts of this energetic young general without diverting forces for the defense of the Papal States. Bonaparte wisely refrained from an attack on Rome itself, perferring to conclude an armistice that cost the Pope

twenty-one million francs, five hundred precious manu-
scripts, and a hundred works of art, the modest beginnings
of the future *Musée Napoléon.*

Having defeated the Austrians at the battle of Rivoli
(January 1797), Bonaparte again exerted pressure on the
Papal States, alleging that Pius had violated the treaty
of the preceding year. The war was the briefest possible,
but the papal treasury suffered a further depletion, this
time nearly double the previous loss. The fortunes of the
papacy—in every sense—were at a low ebb; but after
Bonaparte had sailed for Egypt, a General Duphot was
killed by mistake in a disturbance in Rome, providing the
French with an excuse to occupy the city. On February
20, 1798, the bewildered Pope was arrested, bundled into
a carriage and forcibly taken to Valence in southern
France, where he expired on August 29, 1799. Already
Bologna, Ferrera, and the Romagna had been relinquished
by the Pope, and there was a widespread feeling that the
papacy, as an institution, had run its course and was about
to pass into oblivion.

The conclave to elect a new pope opened in Venice
four months after the death of Pius VI. True, the French
had been forced to abandon Rome, but the Church's precarious finances and the confusion caused by eight years
of war made the election of a pope a difficult matter.
Venice was chosen because the Dean of the Sacred College, Cardinal Albani, was in that city when the Pope
died. The weather was bitterly cold, travel conditions
miserable, and the city, as well as the northern Papal
States, were in the possession of the Emperor Francis of
Austria—hardly the most propitious circumstances. The
balloting dragged on month after month, complicated by
Austrian support of Cardinal Mattei, the man responsible
for having yielded papal territory to General Bonaparte,
a precedent from which Austria hoped to benefit. Mattei's

candidature ran into determined opposition; finally, Cardinal Chiaramonti, Archbishop of Imola, was elected as a compromise. In honor of the deceased pope, he assumed the title of Pius VII.

The choice of the fifty-seven-year-old cardinal was something of a surprise. Like the late Pope, to whom he was greatly indebted, he came from the small city of Cesena, just south of Ravenna. Born of a noble family in 1740, an orphan at the age of eight, Barnabà Gregorio Chiaramonti was a gifted theologian, and promotion came rapidly; after a successful teaching career, he became an abbot, Bishop of Tivoli, and a cardinal, all before the age of forty-three. He was not related to Pius VI, as rumor had it, and his advancement was mainly due to his innate dignity and consideration toward others. At heart he still considered himself a Benedictine monk, and but for the energetic support of Cardinal Consalvi, the secretary of the conclave (and later Pius' personal emissary), he would never have assented to his own elevation to the papal throne. An observant cardinal predicted: "He will be a little Pope in little things. But if the issues become great, he will be as great as they are." He did not have long to wait. The Austrian Emperor was furious at the defeat of his candidate and imperiously summoned the new Pope to Vienna, no doubt to discuss the future of the Papal States. Pius declined the invitation, and perhaps fearing for his life, rather than cross Austrian-held territory by land, he embarked on a pitiable ship down the Adriatic to Pesaro before crossing over to Rome. During his exhausting journey he received the news of Bonaparte's victory at Marengo; henceforth his adversary was not to be the Emperor Francis but the First Consul of the French Republic.

On the face of it, the future of the Church appeared inauspicious. Instead of a Christian monarch, the untested

Pope had to deal with an ambitious general turned political leader. In fact, the prospects for meaningful negotiations were excellent on both sides. Bonaparte, whatever else he was, had never supported the irreligious outbursts of the Revolution, and though his personal theology tended towards the expedient, he saw the need for religion among those he was called upon to rule:

> My policy is to govern men the way the majority wishes. That, I believe, is how one recognizes a people's sovereignty. By becoming Catholic I won the war in the Vendée, by becoming Moslem I established myself in Egypt, and by becoming an ultramontane I won people's hearts in Italy. If I were to rule over a Jewish nation, I would rebuild the Temple of Solomon.

To Bonaparte, revolution divided a nation, whereas religion was a unifying force that inculcated respect for authority; the people should obey their spiritual leaders who, in turn, should look to the First Consul for leadership. As head of the nation, he abhorred the excesses of the Revolution, the division within the French Church, and the rampant anticlericalism. One of his first orders was that elaborate homage be paid to the coffin of the still unburied Pius VI in Valence, a gesture that lent credence to the rumor that the new French government was anxious to discuss the basis of a Concordat with Rome.

Of course, there was also sound political reasoning behind this unexpected *rapprochement*. In his speech to the clergy of Milan on June 5, 1800, the First Consul assured them that only religion could give the State firm and lasting support and that therefore he would reestablish the Church in France. But which of the two factions? This presented no problem, Bonaparte asserting that the Constitutional Church had never been accepted by the people, and that what had been voted in could just as easily be voted out. Only the Pope had authority over the bishops, and therefore it was their sworn duty to obey the Supreme Pontiff. What, at first sight, appeared to be a total capitulation was, in fact, an astute ploy aimed at consolidating the First Consul's position vis-à-vis the monarchists. A Concordat was tantamount to diplomatic recognition of the new régime; and moreover, some valuable concessions might be obtained from Rome that would further strengthen his position. No wonder Bonaparte declared: "If no Pope had existed, it would have been necessary to invent one."

During the campaign of 1797, General Bonaparte and Cardinal Chiaramonti had become acquainted with one another, and when the French advanced through the Papal States, the prelate, rather than seek refuge further south, had remained at his see in Imola. Though he had refused on that occasion to welcome Bonaparte—which could hardly have been expected—on Christmas Day he published a homily that, to conservative ecclesiastics at least, verged on collaboration, if not apostasy. The work, far from being heretical, was a sincere liberal attempt to reconcile the positive aims of the Revolution with Christ's teachings, which, at one time, had also been considered revolutionary. Democracy and the Church, he argued, were in no way incompatible and were indeed complementary to one another:

> The form of democratic government that you have adopted does not clash at all with the Gospel; on the contrary, it demands every sublime virtue which can only be learned at the school of Jesus Christ. . . . Be good Christians, and you will be good democrats.

What is surprising is that the author of this "Jacobin" tract should have been elected Pope two years later.

The discussions in Paris that preceded the signing of the Concordat were protracted and exceedingly complex. Both parties were under great pressures and had to contend with domestic critics hostile to the whole concept. The papacy still had unpleasant memories of the insulting "Conditions for Peace demanded by France from the Court of Rome" of 1796, but thankfully, that demeaning catalogue had been forgotten. Pius did not participate directly in the talks but issued detailed instructions from the Vatican. It was humiliating enough to have to negotiate with apostates like Talleyrand and Fouché; and Cardinal Consalvi, Pius' confidant and Secretary of State, could leave nothing to chance in the company of such devious envoys. Talleyrand succeeded in replacing the reference to a "state religion" by the vaguer phrase that "the Catholic religion . . . was that of a majority of Frenchmen." The ex-Bishop of Autun failed, however, in his attempt to insert a provision that would have allowed married priests (such as himself) to be recognized by the Church. Talleyrand had received strong hints from the First Consul to marry his mistress, the French divorced wife of an Englishman, but the papal negotiators drew the line at including "Madame Grant's Clause" (as it was familiarly known) in the Concordat. The talks dragged on for thirteen months, and at one point Bonaparte threatened to end the matter by becoming a Calvinist and sending Murat's troops into Rome, but finally on July 16, 1801, the document was signed.

The question of the divided church was settled by an ingenious device: the bishops of both factions were to resign *en masse,* thus allowing for an agreement between Bonaparte and Pius to make new appointments in accordance with the new administrative divisions. The Constitutional Clergy submitted meekly, but thirty-seven of the loyalist group—many of them in exile—refused to obey, thus forcing Pius to deprive them of their sees. The Concordat encountered further resistance by its conspicuous omissions and tacit agreements; not a word on the restoration of monasteries, divorce was accepted, and there was to be complete freedom for all religions. Before the agreement was presented to the Legislature, the First Consul added his own list of seventy-seven so-called Organic Articles of which the Vatican was unaware. From these it was clear that the Church was to be subservient to the State, but even so, the vote on April 8, 1802 was by no means unanimous.

The passage of the Concordat left Pius with mixed emotions. The implications of the Organic Articles, the merging of part of the Papal States into the newly-created Italian Republic, the appointment of Bonaparte's uncle, Cardinal Fesch, as Primate of Gaul and later, French Ambassador to the Vatican—all were consequences unpleasant to contemplate. Soon Piedmont became part of France and as such subject to the *Code Napoléon*—divorce south of the Alps!—and Talleyrand's corrupt dealings with the German princes reduced the Church to penury in that country. Yet there were also positive aspects to consider: the Church in France had been saved and a fatal schism averted. Hopefully, the French accord would discourage potential revolutionary upheavals elsewhere, and perhaps a new religious spirit, so wonderfully expressed by Chateaubriand, might prevail instead. These hopes were symbolized by the celebration of Mass in the cathedral of Notre Dame by the papal legate, Cardinal Caprara, on Easter Sunday, 1802. All three Consuls attended, as well as twenty-two bishops and a group of disgruntled generals who were obeying orders with ill grace. The impressive liturgy and music more than made up for the neglected interior of the church and for the occasional scowls of unrepentant revolutionaries.

Napoleon was incapable by nature of viewing life as a placid progress. To him, history had momentum, events were created, opportunities seized. He had long since regarded himself as Charlemagne's successor, he would create a new Empire and have himself crowned by the Pope, not in Rome but in his own capital. He was therefore somewhat incredulous to discover that Pius and Consalvi were determined to win some visible concessions from the newly-proclaimed Emperor before entering into any agreements. Napoleon had become accustomed to the acquiescence of Cardinal Caprara, the papal representative in Paris, so it was embarrassing to learn that Consalvi had even less trouble in outmaneuvering Fesch, the Emperor's own uncle. Pius insisted that all bishops of the ex-Constitutional Church who had been appointed to new sees acknowledge the supremacy of the Pope; Fouché, who had a hand in twelve such appointments, thought it a small price to pay. Napoleon merely observed: "I nominated them, it's up to them to come to terms with the Court of Rome." Thereupon he issued a curt invitation to Pius requesting that he come to Paris without further delay. This aroused the papal wrath, which was vented on an apologetic Fesch.

The Pope had no illusions about the task confronting him. He knew that the Emperor was using the Concordat as an instrument of state policy, that the priests were encouraged to recite *"Domine, salvum fac Napoleonem"* and to lend their support to conscription. Yet Pius was also cognizant that the Church in Rome had failed to keep abreast with the spirit of the times and was remote from the rest of Europe. But he sensed that there was a groundswell, a reaction against the Revolution, a romantic yearning for a more secure past, and that here was an opportunity to present himself to the people as an understanding moral and spiritual leader. Pius was now sixty-one, and the long journey involving the crossing of the Mont Cenis pass and innumerable official receptions would have exhausted many a younger man. One cardinal in the papal entourage died in Lyon, and Pius must have been glad that Consalvi—perhaps anticipating Napoleon's later actions against the Spanish Bourbons at Bayonne—had decided to remain in Rome.

The first meeting with the Emperor at Fontainebleau was a distinct success. Neither man stood on ceremony, and Pius went out of his way to greet everyone, with the conspicuous exception of Madame Talleyrand, the ex-Mrs. Grant. Josephine was acutely aware that, despite the pomp and ceremony, her position was very insecure considering the hostility of the Bonaparte clan and the absence of an heir. She therefore confided to Pius that she strongly doubted the validity of her civil marriage to Napoleon in 1796; there was a question whether the chief witness had been of age, both parties had falsified their ages and other details. Most important of all, no priest had officiated at the wedding. Pius was prepared to dispense with Confession and Communion prior to the Coronation service in Notre Dame, but he would have nothing to do with a couple living in sin. On December 1, Napoleon and Josephine were married in secret by Cardinal Fesch; the next day the Emperor paid the Pope back by crowning both himself and his Empress.

The Vicar of Christ had been publicly humiliated, but the effect was exactly the opposite of that intended. Throughout his stay in Paris, Pius bore himself with a dignity and an unpretentious charm that captivated the crowds that greeted him. His naturalness and obvious sincerity won over many who hitherto had regarded the papacy with hostility, and soon he became so popular that Fouché quietly ordered the press to moderate its praise. Napoleon was furious and refused to make any concessions, but Pius had good reason to feel on his journey home that the Church in France was now in a secure position.

If Napoleon had been married too little, the problem of his brother Jerome was just the opposite. During a youthful escapade he had been married by the Catholic Bishop of Baltimore to an American Protestant, Elizabeth Patterson. Such a mésalliance did not fit in with imperial plans, and despite Jerome's protestations of love, Napoleon ordered him to have his marriage annulled. Cardinal Fesch had assured his nephew that there would be no problem, so the imperial anger was all the greater when the Pope refused to dissolve the union. A penitent Fesch put pressure on the Archbishop of Paris, *et voilà!* in October 1805 the required annulment was granted by the Gallican Church.

The following year, a compliant Cardinal Caprara was easily persuaded to give his assent to the *"catechisme impérial."* Ostensibly a reform aimed at unifying Church teaching, in practice it blurred the division between religion and loyalty to the Emperor, "the Lord's anointed ... raised up by God in a time of trouble." The following is an illustration of the new teaching:

> *Question:* What are the duties of Christians ... towards Napoleon, our Emperor?
> *Answer:* Christians owe to ... Napoleon, our Emperor, love, respect, obedience, loyalty, military service, payment of prescribed levies for the preservation and defense of the Empire and of his throne. We also owe him fervent prayers for his safety and for the spiritual and temporal welfare of the state.

Children were taught that "to honor and serve our Emperor is to honor and serve God himself" and that those who resisted God's order were condemned to eternal damnation. For good measure, April 15 was declared the Feast of St. Napoleon; to those who doubted the new saint's authenticity, the obliging Caprara produced a martyr of the fourth century.

Pius was greatly disheartened by such blatant breaches in the spirit of the Concordat. There was also growing friction on the political level. Napoleon reproached the Pope for tolerating the Protestant English in the southern part of the peninsula, and with this as an excuse, seized the papal port of Ancona on the Adriatic. Angry correspondence followed, and relations rapidly deteriorated. In early December 1805, the Bourbons were chased off the throne of Naples, and direct pressure from Napoleon led to the resignation of Consalvi, supposedly the cause of all the trouble. An added insult was the replacement of the ineffective Fesch by the regicide Alquier as French Ambassador to the Vatican. To underline the new order in what had been the Papal States, on June 5, 1806, General Bernadotte was created Prince of Pontecorvo and—surely the worst indignity of all—Talleyrand was named Prince and Duke of Benevento.

The Pope was clearly on the defensive; but Napoleon's territorial greed—his incursions into Austria, Poland, and especially Spain—placed a formidable weapon in the hands of the Vatican. These lands were deeply Catholic, not merely nominally so as were the majority of Frenchmen, and the threat of excommunication was not to be taken lightly. It was a move that the Emperor genuinely feared, partly, it seems, from nostalgic memories of his religious youth in Corsica. But having acted so far with impunity, he simply could not believe that Pius would invoke the Church's ultimate sanction, and he proceeded to annex further papal territories to the Kingdom of Italy. In January 1808, a handful of French troops occupied Rome, though at first taking care not to disturb the Vatican itself. Within the Church there had been many voices that had seriously doubted the wisdom, even the justifiication, of retaining the anachronistic Papal States, but Rome, the very seat of Christ's Church on earth—no, here Pius would take his stand, no further concession was possible. If the Emperor chose to advance one step more, so be it on his head.

By the spring of 1809 Napoleon had almost completed his plans for the redivision of Italy. Several of his immediate family were rewarded with kingdoms and duchies, while he, with customary modesty, assumed the title of President of the Italian Republic. Only Rome remained, but on May 17, 1809, the omission was rectified by the proclamation that the Holy City would henceforth be part of the French Empire. Napoleon had crossed the Tiber, and Pius had no alternative but to sign the Bull of Excommunication. News of the ban reached Napoleon just prior to the battle of Wagram; regrettably, his instructions, issued in anger, were no more precise than those of Henry II when similarly faced with a "meddlesome prelate." Probably he intended no more than the arrest of Cardinal Pacca, the papal Secretary of State, but General Radet was certain he knew what his Emperor had in mind.

By now, the French had had some experience in kidnapping Popes, but even so, Radet's nocturnal abduction was nearly bungled. Like his predecessor eleven years earlier, Pius was unceremoniously bustled into a waiting carriage and driven north towards Florence where Napoleon's sister Elisa ruled with her ponderous husband. Pius arrived exhausted; the July sun was extremely hot, the windows had been kept closed for fear that he might be recognized, and an axle had broken under the strain of the precipitous rush. A few hours' rest, and the Pontiff was awakened at four in the morning to continue the wild dash to Genoa and across the Alps to Grenoble. Not only had he been separated from Pacca, he was not even allowed to attend Mass on Sunday. Apparently, communications between Napoleon in Austria and those responsible for Pius' safety broke down completely, with the result that the haggard Pope was conducted to Savona on the Mediterranean, this time along the route following the Rhone. Pius was restricted to a suite of five rooms in a monastery, in essence a prisoner cut off from the outside world.

The victory at Wagram opened the way for a dynastic marriage between Napoleon and Marie Louise, the eldest daughter of the Austrian Emperor. After long hesitation and much remorse, Napoleon had come to the regrettable conclusion that a divorce from Josephine could no longer be deferred. This, in turn, raised formidable religious and political problems. Obviously, no sympathetic judgment could be expected from the Head of the Church, even had he been free; and the Emperor Francis regarded the whole matter with repugnance. Once again, the services of Cardinal Fesch, that most obliging of uncles, were required. Having officiated at the religious wedding in person, he could hardly claim that it had never taken place, but he triumphantly discovered that the Council of Trent in the sixteenth century required that the parish priest and two witnesses be present. This condition had not been fulfilled. Furthermore—stretching credibility to its limits—Napoleon had been unaware of the nature of the ceremony and in any case had never given his consent to whatever it was. To Metternich these were trivial details, and he was greatly relieved when the Metropolitan Court of Paris—prodded by Fesch—declared that the religious ceremony was as invalid as the earlier civil service.

Thanks to Fesch's pliant theology, the way was clear for the marriage to Marie Louise. Fesch dutifully blessed the union (as he had that with Josephine) but thirteen other cardinals, led by Consalvi, refused to attend the nuptials. According to Fouché, at one point Napoleon ordered them to be shot, but relented to the extent of depriving them of their benefices and exiling them to the provinces. Meanwhile, the Pope still languished in captivity, dispirited and in poor health, without his counselors or necessary archives. His steadfast refusal to sanction the appointment of new bishops brought much of the administration of the Church to a halt, and even Metternich's personal intervention could not prevail upon Pius to compromise. In mundane matters, there was little he could do when faced with the temporal power of Napoleon, but he was determined to concede as little as possible of his spiritual authority.

For Napoleon, this was a novel and disconcerting experience. In June 1811 he decided to hold a national council of bishops in Paris for the purpose of resolving the irritating question of church appointments. Pius, in his enforced isolation, and weakened, perhaps by drugs administered by a disloyal doctor anxious to see the issue settled, had agreed that the investiture of new bishops could not be delayed indefinitely and had consented to the discussion of certain principles that might resolve the impasse. Fortunately, he did not sign any formal agreement, and as a result, when Napoleon needlessly denigrated Pius before the assembled council, maintaining that the Pontiff had abused his position, he failed to make a convincing case. In fact, he had overplayed his hand, mistaking minor concessions for major weaknesses. He had already achieved most of his aims, but now even the slightest rebuff infuriated him. In a supreme gamble, he demanded Pius' resignation as Pope; though enfeebled by confinement and constant harassment, Pius was still strong in mind and rejected the insulting demand.

A few months later, in June 1812, the Pope, on Napoleon's orders, was conveyed to Fontainebleau in the greatest secrecy. To avoid recognition by friendly crowds, he was forced to travel in the garb of a parish priest. At one point he nearly died, the journey being completed in record time with no halt of more than an hour permitted. The worst part was a wild gallop through Lyon by night on the city cobblestones; Pius simply stated: "May God pardon him since, for my part, I have already pardoned him!" When he finally reached his destination, exhausted and seriously ill, his host was not present to receive him, having embarked on the campaign that was to take him to Moscow. As had happened in Spain, Napoleon learned the impossibility of defeating a people united in defense of their homeland and religion.

On his return to Paris from Russia the defeated Emperor exhibited a spectrum of emotions ranging from unconvincing humility to outright defiance of his encroaching enemies. It was the year of emotional confrontations, including that with Metternich in Dresden. Instead of an eight-hour buffeting, the Pope's ordeal (euphemistically termed a conference) with Napoleon, alternately wheedling and threatening, lasted for six exhausting days. Apparently the Emperor's bullying tactics prevailed, for on January 27, 1813, it was officially announced that a new Concordat had been signed and that all the offending cardinals had been released. On the question of the appointment of bishops, the Pope—fatigued, insulted, and isolated from his entourage—had made an unwilling concession; but soon he had both Consalvi and Pacca on hand to lend him support in the final struggle. On their advice, he sent Napoleon a letter retracting the Concordat as having been obtained under duress. In October, the Emperor was defeated at Leipzig; Fesch, whose skills at extricating Napoleon did not extend to the military, commented, "My nephew is lost, but the Church is saved." For once he had stated a simple truth.

In January 1814 Pius began the first stage of the

journey that would bring him back to Rome after an absence of nearly five years. Napoleon had finally released his illustrious prisoner, ordering him first to be taken back to Savona, and then on to Parma and complete liberty. Now their destinies were reversed; the route to the south coast in a closed carriage would soon be followed by a new captive at Fontainebleau. Chateaubriand, among others, has given us a moving account of the frightened ex-Emperor changing uniforms and disguises to prevent his being recognized by the same crowds that had cheered the passage of the Pope a few weeks previously. It was not quite the end; the Hundred Days served as a dramatic epilogue, and once more Pius was forced to flee the Vatican, though mercifully for but a brief period. Within a few weeks he could return to the Holy See, this time for good.

The narrative is not without its share of ironies. The frail Pope outlived Napoleon by two years, and before his death there was hardly a Bonaparte who did not benefit from his protection and hospitality, including those such as Elisa who had closed their doors to him during that terrible journey in 1809. Even Cardinal Fesch was provided with a palace, which he soon filled with priceless paintings. Having been deprived of his diocese in Lyon, he consoled himself by entertaining on a large scale and participating in the social life of Rome. With characteristic concern, Pius tried to ameliorate the conditions of Napoleon's imprisonment on St. Helena, charitably overlooking his own sufferings at the hands of the Emperor. The Church had survived, its spiritual power enhanced, and for Pius that was reward enough.

Czar
Alexander I

Shortly after the sudden accession of the twenty-four year-old Alexander I to the throne as Czar of All the Russias in 1801, a French spy at the Court in St. Petersburg sent the following eyewitness report to Fouché in Paris: "The young Emperor walks, preceded by the assassins of his grandfather, followed by his father's assassins, and surrounded by his own." Only the last part eventually proved untrue; yet even Alexander's death in 1825 has remained a matter of speculation. A persistent folk legend—supported by the evidence of an empty tomb—has it that the guilt-ridden Czar staged a spurious demise at a remote town on the Black Sea during a serious illness. According to this version, he lived the pious life of a hermit, known for his miraculous gifts, until his death in Siberia in 1864. The most enigmatic and contradictory of all the Czars, idealist and autocrat, mystic

177

and militarist, liberal and reactionary, in Pushkin's phrase, he was "the Sphinx who took his riddle with him to the grave."

No biographer or psychologist has satisfactorily unraveled the complexity of Alexander's tortured character. To his own contemporaries he remained a mystery. Napoleon, who had studied him closely, freely admitted to Metternich: "One could not find a keener mind than that of Emperor Alexander; but I find that there is a piece missing in his character, but for me it is impossible to discover which one." Winston Churchill once remarked that "Russia is a riddle wrapped in a mystery inside an enigma." Alexander further concealed himself behind a religious veil that none could penetrate. Napoleon, schooled in French logic, was ill-equipped to fathom the Russian Sphinx.

Alexander's formative years were tense and disquieting. He was born in 1777 during the liberal reign of his grandmother, Catherine the Great, and his education was entrusted to the care of a Swiss republican, Frédéric-César La Harpe. His formal learning was minimal; nevertheless, he acquired the sensibility and abstract ideas current in the eighteenth century and given political form by the advent of the French Revolution. In 1798 he wrote to La Harpe:

> When my turn comes, we shall have to work little by little to bring into being some kind of National Assembly which, under proper guidance, will prepare a free constitution. After that, my power will cease absolutely and, if God grants me aid, I shall retire into some quiet corner and live happy and at peace.

Contending with the relaxed openness of Catherine's court in St. Petersburg was the martial atmosphere of his father's world at the Little Court of Gatchina, some twenty miles distant from the capital. Catherine's son,

Paul, was a martinet, an open admirer of Prussian military discipline, to which he added a sadistic streak of cruel punishments and relentless parade ground drilling. The young Alexander shuttled between both courts, adapting himself with apparent ease to the two extremes; throughout life. he remained equally adept at discussing the merits of a constitution as in delighting at the precision of a well-executed maneuver. His gracious, upright bearing seemed to many the felicitous assimilation of two opposite modes of life; more discerning observers might have attributed it rather to an early gift for dissimulation.

Catherine detested her son to the same extent that she adored her grandson. Alexander was handsome, above average in stature, a delightful conversationalist who charmed his interlocutors by his enthusiasm and seeming sincerity. Though slightly deaf (due to his father's incessant cannonades), in the eyes of many this was the only flaw in their perfect prince, who appeared to be happily married to Elisabeth, a German princess from Baden. The Empress Catherine was determined to ignore the rightful claims of the Czarevitch Paul in favor of Alexander, but before she could promulgate her imperial wish, she was overtaken by death.

Czar Paul's brief reign is chiefly remembered for its brutality, arbitrary decrees, and terror. Soon his irrational behavior, often verging on madness, engendered that most Russian of solutions, a conspiracy that led directly to his assassination during the night of March 23, 1801. Alexander had foreknowledge of the plot, but had pleaded that his father's life be spared, otherwise keeping the secret to himself. Though at most a tacit accessory, he soon convinced himself that he was a patricide and that the Fates would deny his soul a moment's rest. He was immediately proclaimed Czar Alexander I; it was given out that Paul had died of an apoplectic stroke, which prompted Talleyrand to remark that "the Russians ought to invent another illness to explain the death of their emperors."

The first months of Alexander's reign aroused fervent expectations throughout the country. Unlike his father, the new Czar was an early admirer of Bonaparte and regarded him as the savior of France and Christianity by virtue of the recently concluded Concordat. Both men had acceded to power by force and both felt an urgent need to prove themselves to their own people. Through the creation of the Unofficial Committee, Alexander gathered around him a group of outstanding liberal minds; a Charter of the Russian People and the abolition of serfdom were discussed at length, but no decision was taken. Though minor reforms were instituted at the universities and censorship was curtailed, the old autocratic tradition gradually reasserted itself once Alexander felt reasonably secure on his throne. His liberal ideas were dreams with little substance or support, consistently undermined by a languid *Weltschmerz*. Cecil elucidates the process:

> An idea with the Russian Emperor would take two years to germinate, and would, in the third year, bear fruit, only in the fourth to be wearied of and condemned as noxious, and in the fifth to be left to wither away. Thus his life, which abounded in purposes, had never purpose.... He was, in fact, a politician of the most pathetic school—a visionary continuously losing hope and learning fear. Having proved all things and held fast to none, having consorted first with liberals and idealogues and finally with conservatives and mystics, he, whose sovereign power was supreme and unchallenged, came at the end, as Metternich declares, to die from weariness of life.

Initially, the same optimism prevailed in foreign affairs. Reversing his father's expansionist policies, Alexander ordered the recall of an expeditionary force headed for India and patched up relations with England. In an idealistic vein he hoped to prevail on Bonaparte to withdraw from some of the conquered territories, thus naïvely hoping to assure peace throughout Europe. A treaty with France was signed in October 1801, but it was not long before Alexander was branding the First Consul and Talleyrand as "scoundrels" for having disregarded the terms and spirit of the agreement. Though hesitant at first, the young Czar was gradually becoming aware of Bonaparte's true nature and the problems confronting Russia.

The judicial murder of the duc d'Enghien in March 1804 struck a particularly vulnerable spot in Alexander's sensitive mind. Nearly alone among Europe's monarchs, he vigorously denounced the callous spilling of royal blood by a rank commoner. In his protest he chose to overlook the murky history of the Romanov dynasty, including the violent event that had enabled him but three years previously to ascend the throne. Bonaparte in his official reply, which appeared in the *Moniteur,* was less considerate, posing the not-so-hypothetical question of what the Russian government would have done at the time of Czar Paul's assassination had it discovered the conspirators within a league of the national frontier. Less than two months later, the First Consul proclaimed himself Emperor, thus placing himself on the same level as the Czar. Alexander never forgave these personal insults, and henceforth bent all his energies toward the ultimate destruction of Napoleon.

Though he refused to recognize the new French Emperor—least of all his claim to be the successor of Charlemagne—Alexander reluctantly conceded (if only to himself) that France and Russia were the only two countries with sane rulers. By a cruel coincidence, the remaining monarchies were afflicted by madness and other infirmities too numerous or disreputable to mention. Increasingly, Alexander came to regard himself and Napoleon as antagonists in an ineluctable conflict, an historic duel that would have to be fought out *mano a mano*. Seen in this light, it was a short step to viewing himself as God's chosen champion in the struggle against the usurper. Napoleon had just crowned himself in Milan as King of Italy following his coronation in Paris; might he not cast covetous eyes towards the Russian throne? Clearly, it was the Czar's sacred duty to thwart such godless ambitions, and with Austria as his sole reliable ally, he took to the field.

The duality of Alexander's character soon manifested itself. In his role as crusader, he prayed at the tomb of Frederick the Great; as Emperor, he conversed with Goethe in Weimar before rejoining his army. Ignoring the cautious advice of the elderly General Kutuzov to avoid a pitched battle with Napoleon, Alexander's overconfidence was such as to permit General Savary to visit the Russian headquarters and report back to his Emperor! Austerlitz was an unmitigated disaster; the hours of parade ground drilling could not disguise the military unpreparedness of the army as defeat turned to rout. The Czar wept openly, shaken in spirit by the magnitude of the French victory and his own inability to do other than join his soldiers in headlong flight. Back in St. Petersburg he was openly reviled, even by his own mother, the Dowager Empress. Alexander was held directly responsible for the nation's misfortune, and for several weeks thereafter remained a recluse from the public.

After Prussia's defeat by Napoleon in 1806, a campaign which removed the main protective barrier between France and Russia, few doubted that further war could be averted. Undeniably, Napoleon was admired in certain circles in St. Petersburg and elsewhere, but the majority of Russians followed the lead of the Orthodox Church, which had officially declared the French Emperor to be the Enemy of Religion. Furthermore, the dishonor of Austerlitz called for revenge. At the battle of Eylau, Napoleon was nearly defeated by General Bennigsen, but the subsequent disaster at Friedland (June 14, 1807) resulted in a reversal of public opinion, depriving Alexander of the necessary public support to continue the war. Humiliated by Napoleon (who scurrilously insinuated that the Czar had only fought in the first place to obtain the favors of the attractive Queen of Prussia), Alexander was forced to accede to a face-to-face meeting with his adversary at Tilsit. The fickleness and inconsistency of the Court was such that the Czar was roundly criticized for holding pourparlers with the "accursed Frenchman"; in the eyes of his courtiers, many of whom insisted on speaking French among themselves (as Tolstoy emphasized in *War and Peace*), whatever he did was wrong. That Alexander might be gaining a valuable respite for his country did not occur to them.

For the thirteen days of discussions and social events at Tilsit, Napoleon adopted the role of magnanimous victor and solicitous host. At the zenith of his power, he dazzled Alexander by conjuring up a vision of Russia's "civilizing hand" bringing order to a degenerate Turkish Empire that had just deposed the Sultan. After annexing Constantinople, perhaps the Czar might liberate Orthodox Greece from her Muslim oppressors. The talks, held on a raft moored in the middle of the Nieman river, in a tent bearing the initials of the two sovereigns, were entirely informal; Napoleon joked that "I'll be your secretary, and you will be mine." On another occasion, to justify the exclusion of the Austrian Emperor, with heavy humor he observed that "I've often slept two to a bed, never three."

The two men soon were expressing the highest regard for one another. Noting the modesty of Alexander's quarters, Napoleon graciously insisted on providing him with more suitable accommodations in the town of Tilsit. The two Emperors were seen walking along arm in arm in intimate conversation, the bloody battlefield of a fortnight ago all but forgotten. Napoleon, believing that he had gained complete ascendancy over the impressionable Czar, sought to establish a personal relationship which would not only be more effective than a formal treaty but also less binding. Thus, their chats tended to be philosophical, enlivened with anecdotes and reminiscences, such as Napoleon's accounts of his first victories; these were interspersed with gratuitous lessons in the art of warfare from the master. On a more intimate level, the Emperor spoke about his family and the bereavement that Queen Hortense, his sister-in-law, had just suffered through the death of her son. Alexander proved to be a sympathetic listener, and Napoleon had every reason to believe that he had conquered Russia without a battle.

But had he? Certainly the terms of the peace treaty signed on July 7, 1807, appeared favorable to France; the Czar promised to adhere to the Continental Blockade directed against England, and France gained certain strategic posts in the Mediterranean. To judge by the fraternization among the officers and soldiers, the generous distribution of medals and honors, the emotional pledges of friendship given by both sides, one might have thought that the Tilsit summit meeting had assured peace for years to come. Yet this was all a façade, an empty pretense. Behind Alexander's slavic charm hid a byzantine mind, and soon he was confiding to a friend, "if the circumstances change, then policy can also change." Napoleon's basic assumption was that he had fully understood every nuance of Alexander's mind, every mood of the "Talma of the North," as he called him. It was a fatal miscalculation.

Having divided up the continent into mutual spheres of influence (Prussia and—as usual—Poland were the main losers), the two Emperors bade one another an elaborate and cordial farewell. Left behind were the lies, hypocrisy, and secret articles in the treaty, which proved to be as meaningless as the contrived meeting itself. Once again, Alexander had to face the ill-concealed hostility of St. Petersburg society for having humiliated himself before the French tyrant. When Savary was sent by Napoleon as his Ambassador to Russia—a most infelicitous choice, considering his direct part in the Enghien affair —he was snubbed on all sides, rendering his diplomatic mission virtually impossible. His successor, Armand de Caulaincourt, was so overwhelmed by Alexander's charm and apparent sincerity as to seriously reduce his effectiveness. In Paris, the situation was the reverse, thanks to a well-placed spy at the Ministry of War and to the occasional hints dropped by Talleyrand. Napoleon soon became convinced that another meeting with the Czar was imperative.

During the year following the Tilsit honeymoon, a more objective reassessment had taken place on both sides. The correspondence between the two Emperors showed no diminution in hollow flattery, as Napoleon's letter to Alexander in the spring of 1808 indicates:

> Your Majesty and I would have preferred the gentleness of peace and spending our lives in the midst of our vast empires, busy giving them new life and making them happy through the arts and the benefits of administration. Our enemies in the world won't allow it. We must be greater in spite of ourselves. It is wisdom and statecraft to fulfill what Destiny commands and to go wherever the irresistible march of events leads us. . . .

In May of the same year, the "irresistible march" led the French Emperor to Madrid; to his dismay, the Spanish patriots stubbornly refused to play the docile role he had assigned them. Despite the setback at Bailén, he was convinced that Spain could be defeated within three months, perhaps even before the meeting with Alexander at Erfurt in September. What Napoleon was totally unaware of were the combined efforts of Talleyrand and Caulaincourt to strengthen Alexander's resolve to win a peace settlement based on a discussion between equals rather than a continuation of Russia's undignified position as subservient ally.

Just at this time an event, more suited to *petite histoire* than to the momentous meetings of heads of state, was taking place in the background. Alexander's marriage had failed, and he and the Empress Elisabeth had become estranged from one another. The Czar had found solace with a Polish princess, conveniently married to an understanding Russian nobleman who generously sympathized with his Emperor's predicament. Maria Naryshkina soon gained a dangerous ascendancy over Alexander, so much so that Napoleon (who had meanwhile acquired a Polish mistress of his own) became concerned over the possible political implications. Previously, along with many others, Napoleon had enjoyed the favors of Mlle George, a famous actress of the day. Having tired of her charms, he had left her in search of other feminine companionship. In any case, Mlle George left Paris on May 7, 1808, and arrived in St. Petersburg in early June to an enthusiastic welcome. The French historian Masson claims that she was dispatched (probably by Napoleon) as a counter-attraction to the alluring Maria. If this was the covert intention, it unexpectedly failed; the whole affair—or, more accurately, lack thereof—came to an end when Alexander gallantly presented the actress with a generous gift before she departed the capital in January, 1813.

The proposed meeting with Napoleon at Erfurt was

as strongly opposed in court circles as the earlier conference in Tilsit. Many feared that the French were pre-
paring a trap similar to that sprung on the hapless Spanish
royal family at Bayonne and that Alexander would become Napoleon's captive. Others, less concerned with the
Czar's personal fate, considered him to be little more than
the tool of the French. Most observers had failed to remark a decisive change in Alexander's attitude towards
the Corsican Colossus; to one of his advisers he confided,
"let us appear to be his dupe but without being so." Even
before the two Emperors met, Talleyrand hastened to
flatter Alexander on his arrival at Erfurt: "Sire, what are
you going to do here? It is your task to save Europe, and
you will only succeed by being firm with Napoleon. The
French people are civilized, but not their sovereign; the
Russian sovereign is civilized, but not his people. It is
therefore the duty of the Russian sovereign to be the ally
of the French people." Once the opening pleasantries
were dispensed with, it soon became evident to Napoleon
that Alexander was no longer the puppet of Tilsit.

The meeting at Erfurt (September 28-October 14,
1808) was a further exercise in mutual duplicity, but
with a shift in emphasis: Alexander, buoyed by Talleyrand's intrigues, proved unexpectedly stubborn. Beneath
the courteous exterior of the Czar, Napoleon was quick
to discern a lack of trust, an unwillingness to accept
French assurances at their face value. As before, Napoleon dominated the conversation, while Alexander
listened patiently with few interruptions or ripostes. It
was all the more infuriating to discover that an impassioned torrent of words had made no impression on his
interlocutor, who, with a gentle smile, adhered to his
original position. This quiet, but firm, resistance caused
Napoleon to complain to his Ambassador, Caulaincourt:
"Your Emperor Alexander is as stubborn as a mule; he

pretends to be deaf when he does not want to understand."
One day, exasperated by such tactics, Napoleon threw
his hat on the ground and stamped on it. Alexander
smiled, then remarked: "You are violent and I am ob-
stinate: with me, anger won't get you anywhere. Let's
talk and reason, otherwise I am leaving." Napoleon had
tried in vain to secure Russia as an active ally in a war
against Austria, but finally had to settle for an unconvincing promise of help in case of hostilities.

On the surface, the fraternal spirit evidenced at Tilsit
continued. The two Emperors went on a literary pilgrimage to Weimar and visited the battlefield at Jena,
besides attending classical French plays together. One
evening, during a performance of Voltaire's *Oedipe*, on
hearing the famous verse, *"L'amitié d'un grand homme
est un bienfait des dieux"* (The friendship of a great man
is a favor from the gods), Alexander rose and spontane-
ously grasped Napoleon's hand. On another occasion,
Napoleon offered the Czar his sword as a gift, whereupon
Alexander graciously replied: "I shall never draw it
against Your Majesty." Despite such testimonials of mutual respect, the underlying reality was not so assuring.
Rumors that Napoleon might be seeking a wife of royal
birth had been current for several months; Alexander's
favorite sister Catherine had been frequently mentioned
in this connection. At Erfurt, the Czar did nothing to
facilitate such a union, no decision was taken, and a week
after his return to St. Petersburg the marriage of
Catherine to the heir of the Duchy of Oldenburg was
announced.

On October 14, the two Emperors took leave of one
another, never to meet again. Alexander has been criticized by some historians for not having extracted more
favorable terms from the meeting. The facts, however, in-
dicate that the Czar played his diplomatic hand extremely

well. He knew that Napoleon had yet to lose a major battle, and the defeat that Austria sustained the following year at Wagram confirmed his contention that the time to confront the French on the battlefield had not yet arrived. The Russian armies "hurried slowly" to aid their French ally, carefully avoiding any conflict, much to Napoleon's displeasure. Nor was Russian assistance in the marital field any more pronounced; Alexander pleaded that his sister Anna was as yet too young to marry Napoleon, that the Dowager Empress would have to approve the union (an unlikely event), and suggested that an interim wait of two years might be advisable. Napoleon saw through Alexander's obvious stratagem, and without further delay took measures to secure the hand of Marie Louise. The invasion of Russia was now only a matter of time.

Not only was the Tilsit honeymoon over, but also any romantic notion based on eternal friendship between the two heads of state. Diplomatic frictions, hitherto avoided, now became commonplace as both countries prepared for the inevitable struggle. Michael Speransky, who, in his attempt to reform the bureaucratic and financial structure of Russia had not hesistated to borrow French ideas where applicable, fell from power in early 1812. The formidable task of reorganizing the army was entrusted to Count Arakcheyev, a harsh disciplinarian generally hated, but a trusted friend of Alexander's from the Gatchina days. The Russian officer corps, severely depleted at Austerlitz and Friedland, received considerable replenishment from Prussian career soldiers, among whom was the brilliant strategist von Clausewitz. In the courts and ministries throughout Europe, the coming war and the strategy to be employed were the animated topics of the day.

Typically, Alexander vacillated between protestations

of loyalty to Napoleon and displays of defiance. In late 1810 he unilaterally abrogated Russia's adherence to the Continental System, whereupon Napoleon retaliated by annexing the Duchy of Oldenburg, whose ruler was related to Alexander through marriage to the latter's sister Catherine. In Naples, the Russian and French envoys fought a duel, while in Paris Napoleon directed a calculated tirade at the nonplussed Russian Ambassador. Caulaincourt, meanwhile, had attempted to provide his master with an accurate assessment of Alexander's growing determination to resist to the end, quoting his words: "I would rather retreat to Kamchatka than surrender my territory and sign in my capital an agreement that anyway will only be a temporary truce." The Czar had assured the departing French Ambassador that Russia did not desire a war and would not fire the first shot; "however, if we are attacked, we shall know how to defend ourselves." Napoleon contemptuously rejected such utterances out of hand—"one good battle will knock the bottom out of my friend Alexander's fine resolutions." On May 16, 1812, Napoleon arrived in Dresden, convinced that an imposing display of military strength might well prove sufficient to cow the Russians into submission without a battle.

The festivities at Dresden, the impressive array of crowned heads and military parades, all recalled the same orchestrated effects that had awed onlookers at Erfurt, except, of course, that Czar Alexander was no longer one of the principal participants. In an effort to appear conciliatory, Napoleon sent Count de Narbonne, Minister of War during the reign of Louis XVI (and Mme de Staël's ex-lover), to Alexander, who received him courteously, but firmly, with the measured reply: "I know how great a military leader Napoleon is, but on my side I have space and time.... I will not start the war, but I will not disarm so long as a single enemy soldier remains in Russia." At the same time, Alexander concluded peace with Turkey, thus releasing an additional army for the defense of the homeland. When the *Grande Armée* of over half a million men drawn from nearly every nation in Europe crossed the Nieman into Russia, few comprehended where Napoleon was leading them.

The news of the invasion reached the Czar during a ball given at the country home of General Bennigsen, one of several Russian senior officers of foreign origin. Alexander was still anxious to avert hostilities, and accordingly sent a personal envoy, General Balashov, to Napoleon with the message that, "if Your Majesty consents to retire his troops from Russian territory, I shall regard what has happened as null and void, and an accommodation is still possible between us." Napoleon could barely contain his anger at Alexander's impertinence. The fool! To expect the victor of Austerlitz and Friedland to withdraw without a single battle! Having regained his composure, he heavy-handedly asked the Russian envoy which was the best route to Moscow. Balashov replied that there were several, but that Charles XII of Sweden had chosen the road through Poltava—the scene of his great defeat. Napoleon's fury reasserted itself; these cowardly Russian generals refused to offer battle and persisted in retreating towards the interior. Already his army stretched for miles, suffering alternately from the dust, rain, and summer heat, while the tenuous supply lines soon proved inadequate. This wasn't war—Alexander was mocking him by refusing to adhere to the traditional rules. Napoleon, it seems, had learned very little from his Spanish incursion.

The Russians, however, were not without their problems. Many resented the sacrifice of their properties and the national ignominy of constant withdrawal. A coherent strategy was not helped by the petty bickering among generals, some of whom spoke Russian with a heavy accent or not at all. Only on one point was there common accord: with memories still fresh of Alexander's disastrous personal intervention at Austerlitz, he was prevailed upon to retire first to Moscow, where he received a surprisingly enthusiastic welcome, and then to St. Petersburg, where, despite a noticeably restrained reception, he remained for the duration of the war. With great reluctance he appointed the elderly General Kutuzov as commander-in-chief, at least a Russian by birth and one who commanded the respect and loyalty of the soldiers.

For a man of Alexander's sensitive nature, the weeks of inaction forced upon him were a severe ordeal. Many of his entourage, even within his own family, wavered in their resolve on hearing of the destruction of Smolensk. Shortly before, Alexander had been fortified by the reassuring words of Mme de Staël. Together they condemned Napoleon's machinations before indulging in a frenzy of mutual flattery, Germaine at her wits' end to enumerate all of Alexander's outstanding virtues. In a more somber mood, his introspective nature embraced a religious mysticism that convinced him that Holy Russia was engaged in a crusade against the atheistic French. Having assured the English representative that he would resist to the end, he added: "I would sooner let my beard grow to the waist and eat potatoes in Siberia." Alexander's resolve was unshakable; despite the carnage at Borodino, the burning of Moscow, nothing would deter him from his God-given task to free his land from the foreigner. Turning to Kutuzov, Alexander averred: "It's Napoleon or me! We can no longer reign together. I have learned to know him; he will no longer deceive me!" In vain Napoleon waited for the Czar's offer to negotiate; it never came.

The details of the painful retreat are too well-known to bear retelling. When the last bedraggled remnants of the *Grande Armée* recrossed the Nieman, the majority of the Czar's advisers were content to terminate Russia's part in the war against Napoleon. By now, Alexander was moved by a deep desire to imbue any European peace settlement with Christian principles; accordingly, he decided that the war against the anti-Christ must be vigorously prosecuted until final victory. Those who had known the Czar for many years were amazed at his resilience, even when the Allies suffered two reverses in the spring of 1813. Alexander was fond of quoting the maxim that he had heard from Napoleon's own lips at Erfurt: " 'In war, it is tenacity that counts for everything; that is how I have always been victorious.' ... Well then, I'll prove to him that I have not forgotten his lessons." At the battle of Leipzig which sealed Napoleon's fate, it was the inspiring presence of the Czar on the battlefield that rallied his forces. During the action, Alexander narrowly avoided being killed by a hostile cannon ball; surely here was tangible proof that God had chosen him as His instrument.

The final months of the war became increasingly a direct confrontation—in spirit, if not face to face—between Czar and Emperor. The Allies were disheartened by a series of brilliant tactical victories gained by Napoleon on French soil; again, it was Alexander's determination that prevailed and carried the invading armies to Paris. Far from being vindictive—it had been feared the Russians might destroy the French capital—Alexander delighted the Parisians by his generosity and solicitude. The Czar, mounted on an Arabian charger presented to him by Napoleon at Erfurt, entered the city to the acclaim of *"Vive l'empereur Alexandre!"* Not only were there no reprisals, but the majority of local officials continued in their posts. He further endeared himself to the populace by tactfully declining to take up residence in the Tuileries with its memories of Napoleon (to whom he offered a domicile in Russia) and of the Bourbons (whom he collectively despised). It required all of Talleyrand's persuasive powers to convince Alexander that the royal principle of legitimacy was all-important and therefore, Louis XVIII must ascend the throne of his ancestors.

Alexander was at the pinnacle of his power, the first time that a Russian ruler had been pre-eminent in Europe. This was the opportunity to transform religious conviction into political reality; and with these pious thoughts in mind, the Czar approached his fellow monarchs and their skeptical ministers. Against such a background he sought to present his point of view: "Napoleon's fall is not only an imperative political necessity; it is further required by Christian conscience as an example of justice and morality for the world to behold." Unfortunately, Alexander's vision of a Holy Alliance as the basis of future conduct between nations foundered on the indifference of cynical diplomats; his cool reception in London and his later eclipse in Vienna reflected the harsh, practical reality. Even Louis XVIII humiliated him at an official dinner. Marie Louise and Josephine—each of whom, in her own way, had loved Napoleon—were among the few who showed the dejected Czar any true respect now that the wave of adulation had expended itself. It was during an evening walk with Alexander at Malmaison that Josephine caught a severe chill; within a few hours she was dead.

The remaining ten years of his reign witnessed the collapse of all his cherished hopes. A weariness of spirit became increasingly evident, curiously juxtaposed between a pervasive mysticism and an assertive autocracy.

At times he could still display the same generous qualities that had once fascinated those who came in contact with him. Napoleon, on his return from Elba, discovered a document attesting to the perfidious conduct of the Allies towards Alexander. At once it was rushed to the Czar in Vienna; but, having first vented his anger on reading the incriminating evidence, he then calmly confronted Metternich with the query: "Are you familiar with this document?" Cutting short the stammerings of the Austrian minister, Alexander continued: "Metternich, as long as we live, let there be no mention of this between us. At the moment we have other things to do. Let us only think about our alliance against Napoleon." Suiting action to the word, he tossed the offending sheet of paper into the fire.

Because of the geographical dispersal of the Russian armies, Alexander played little part in the Waterloo campaign. His second entry into Paris was in marked contrast to the first; the populace showed an understandable reluctance to commit itself in the light of recent events. And the Czar was wary of the fickle crowd which had once greeted him so enthusiastically, yet within a year had equally acclaimed Napoleon on his return from Elba. In September 1815, Alexander made a grandiose attempt to overawe his detractors by the strength of his vision. His penchant for military parades was as strong as ever, and on the extensive plain of Vertus, near Châlons, he took the salute as the Russian army—some 180,000 men—marched in perfect formation past the invited kings and generals. The next day, the feast of Saint Alexander, a magnificent *Te Deum* was celebrated at seven altars set among the soldiers to herald the consecration of the Holy Alliance and, hopefully, the inauguration of a new era.

Fittingly, one of the last receptions that Alexander

attended in Paris took place at the residence of Mme Krüdener, whose religious influence over the Czar was paramount during this period. Among other guests were Mme de Staël, her close friend Mme Récamier, an admiring Benjamin Constant, and a newly stirred Chateaubriand. Each had suffered under Napoleon, and now they found themselves in the presence of the northern mystic who, more than any other individual, had brought down the oppressor. No doubt they were perplexed by the Czar's protean nature and at a loss to explain his ambivalent actions, but all were charmed by his graciousness and sincerity.

In later years, Chateaubriand concluded that, "after Bonaparte, Alexander is the greatest historical figure of the Napoleonic era"; but in a partial retraction, he also described him as a "strong soul and a feeble character." He might have added that the Czar, in his own way, was the embodiment of the aspirations and contradictions of his age, encouraging the liberal hopes of his early years but allowing the later repressive measures that led directly to the Decembrist revolution a few weeks after his death. But perhaps Alexander did not die in that isolated community by the Black Sea; like Napoleon, he lives forever in the imagination of each succeeding generation.

Bibliography

The following is a list of the source material used in the preparation of this book. I have purposely omitted the voluminous literature on Napoleon himself, which, in most cases, deals only indirectly with the subject matter treated in the present work and adds little to a further understanding of these personages.

Adhemar, Jean. *Goya*. Paris: Pierre Tisné, 1948.

Alcalá Galiano, Antonio. *Recuerdos de un anciano*. Buenos Aires: Espasa-Calpe, 1951.

Almedingen, E. M. *The Emperor Alexander I*. New York: The Vanguard Press, n.d.

Andrews, Wayne. *Germaine: A Portrait of Madame de Staël*. New York: Atheneum, 1963.

Baldick, Robert. *The Memoirs of Chateaubriand*. New York: Alfred A. Knopf, 1961.

Bibliography

Berger, Morroe. *Madame de Staël on Politics, Literature, and National Character.* New York: Doubleday & Co., 1964.

Bibl, Viktor. *Metternich.* Vienna: Johannes Günther Verlag, 1936.

Brandt, Otto. *August Wilhelm Schlegel, Der Romantiker und die Politik.* Stuttgart and Berlin: Deutsche Verlags-Anstalt, 1919.

Cecil, Algernon. *Metternich.* London: Eyre & Spottiswoode, 1947.

Chastenet, Jacques. *Godoy, Master of Spain 1792-1808.* London: The Batchworth Press, 1953.

Chateaubriand, François René de. *Mémoires d'Outre-Tombe.* Paris: Gallimard, 1951.

Cole, Hubert. *Fouché, The Unprincipled Patriot.* London: Eyre & Spottiswoode, 1971.

Constant, Benjamin. *Mémoires sur les Cent-Jours.* Paris: Pichon et Didier, 1829.

————. *Adolphe.* Paris: Editions Garnier Frères, n.d.

————. *Adolphe* and *The Red Note Book,* with an Introduction by Harold Nicolson. Indianapolis-New York: The Bobbs-Merrill Company, Inc., 1959.

————. *Benjamin Constant.* Actes du Congrès de Lausanne (October 1967). Geneva: Librairie Droz, 1968.

Cordey, Pierre. *Madame de Staël et Benjamin Constant sur les bords du Léman.* Lausanne: Payot, 1966.

Corona Baratech, Carlos. *Revolución y Reacción en el Reinado de Carlos IV.* Madrid: Ediciones Rialp, 1957.

Correard, F. *La France sous le Consulat.* Paris: Société Française d'éditions d'art, n.d.

Cubberly, Ray Ellsworth. *The Role of Fouché during the Hundred Days.* Madison: University of Wisconsin Press, 1969.

D'Auvergne, Edmund. *Godoy, the Queen's Favourite.* Boston: The Gorham Press, 1913.

De Salas, Xavier, and Fauré, Elie. *The Disasters of War.* 85 aquatint etchings by Goya. New York: Anchor Books, Doubleday & Co., 1956.

du Gué Trapier, Elizabeth. *Goya and His Sitters: A Study of his Style as a Portraitist.* New York: Hispanic Society of America, 1964.

Dupuis, G., et al. *Chateaubriand ou la Fidélité Politique.* Paris: Armand Colin, 1967.

Forssell, Nils. *Fouché, The Man Napoleon Feared.* London: George Allen & Unwin, Ltd., 1928.

Fouché, Joseph. *Mémoires.* New York: Sturgis & Walton Co., 1912.

Fugier, André. *Napoléon et l'Espagne.* (2 vols.) Paris: Librairie Félix Alcan, 1930.

Godoy, Manuel. *Memorias* (Biblioteca de Autores Españoles 88, 89. Edición y estudio preliminar de Carlos Seco Serrano). Madrid: BAE, 1956.

Guillemin, Henri. *Madame de Staël, Benjamin Constant et Napoléon.* Paris: Librairie Plon, 1959.

Hales, E. E. Y. *The Emperor and the Pope.* New York: Doubleday & Co., 1961.

Harris, Enriqueta. *Goya.* London: Phaidon Press Ltd., 1969.

Herold, Christopher J. *Mistress to an Age: A Life of Madame de Staël.* Indianapolis-New York: The Bobbs-Merrill Company, Inc., 1958.

Herr, Richard. *The Eighteenth-Century Revolution in Spain.* Princeton: Princeton University Press, 1958.

Heyer, Friedrich. *The Catholic Church from 1648 to 1870.* London: Adam & Charles Black, 1969.

Holdheim, William W. *Benjamin Constant.* New York: Hillary House Publishers, 1961.

Huch, Ricarda. *Die Romantik: Blütezeit, Ausbreitung, Verfall.* Tübingen: Rainer Wunderlich Verlag, 1951.

Bibliography

Izquierdo Hernández, Manuel. *Antecedentes y Comienzos del Reinado de Fernando VII.* Madrid: Ediciones Cultura Hispánica, 1963.

Jaeck, Emma Gertrude. *Madame de Staël and the Spread of German Literature.* New York: Oxford University Press, American Branch, 1915.

Kraehe, Enno, ed. *The Metternich Controversy.* New York: Holt, Rinehart & Winston, 1971.

Lovett, Gabriel. *Napoleon and the Birth of Modern Spain* (2 vols.). New York: New York University Press, 1965.

Madol, Hans Roger. *Godoy.* Madrid: Alianza Editorial, 1966.

Marti, Francisco. *El proceso del Escorial.* Pamplona: Universidad de Navarra, 1965.

Maurois, André. *Chateaubriand.* New York and London: Harper & Row, 1938.

McConnell, Allen. *Tsar Alexander I, Paternalistic Reformer.* New York: Thomas Y. Crowell, 1970.

Melchior-Bonnet, Christian, ed. *Napoléon par Chateaubriand.* Paris: Editions Albin Michel, 1969.

Metternich, Klement. *Mémoires.* Paris: E. Plon et Cie., 1880.

Nicolson, Harold. *Benjamin Constant.* London: Constable Publishers, 1949.

Paléologue, Maurice. *Alexandre Ier, Un Tsar Enigmatique.* Paris: Librairie Plon, 1937.

Palmer, Alan. *Metternich.* New York: Harper & Row, 1972.

_____. *Napoleon in Russia.* London: André Deutsch, 1967.

Pange, Comtesse Jean de. *Auguste-Guillaume Schlegel et Madame de Staël.* Paris: Editions Albert, 1938.

Robiquet, Jean. *La vie quotidienne au temps de Napoléon.* Paris: Hachette, 1938.

Rodríguez, Alfred. *An Introduction to the Episodios Nacionales of Galdós.* New York: Las Américas Publishing Company, 1967.

Sauvigny, Bertier de. *Metternich et son temps.* Paris: Hachette, 1959.

Schickel, Richard. *The World of Goya.* New York: Time-Life Books, 1968.

Spiel, Hilde. *The Congress of Vienna.* Philadelphia: Chilton Book Company, 1968.

Srbik, Heinrich von. *Metternich* (2 vol.). Munich: Verlag F. Bruckmann KG, 1957.

Staël-Holstein, Germaine. *Ten Years' Exile.* Fontwell, Sussex: Centaur Press, n.d.

Staiger, Emil, ed. *August Wilhelm Schlegels Kritische Schriften.* Zürich: Artemis Verlag, 1962.

Stephens, Winifred. *Women of the French Revolution.* London: Chapman and Hall, 1922.

Strakhovsky, Leonid. *Alexander I of Russia: The Man who defeated Napoleon.* New York: W. W. Norton & Co., 1947.

Switzer, Richard, ed. *Chateaubriand Today.* Madison: University of Wisconsin Press, 1970.

Turquan, Joseph. *Madame de Staël, sa vie amoureuse, politique et mondaine.* Paris: Editions Emile-Paul Frères, 1926.

Vallentin, Antonina. *This I Saw: The Life and Times of Goya.* New York: Random House, 1949.

Vallotton, Henri, *Le Tsar Alexandre Ier.* Paris: Editions Berger-Levrault, 1966.

Vandal, Albert. *Napoléon et Alexandre Ier.* (3 vol.). Paris: Librairie Plon, 1906.

Verbist, Henri, *Les grandes controverses de l'Eglise contemporaine 1789-1965.* Lausanne: Editions Rencontre, 1969.

Bibliography

Walker, Mack. *Metternich's Europe*. New York: Walker & Co., 1968.

Walzel, Oskar. *German Romanticism*. New York: Capricorn Books, 1966.

Woodward, E. L. *Three Studies in European Conservatism*. New York: Archon Books, 1963.

Zabala y Lera, Pío. *España bajo los Borbones*. Barcelona: Editorial Labor, S.A., 1945.

Zweig, Stefan. *Joseph Fouché, The Portrait of a Politician*. New York: The Viking Press, 1930.

Index

The name of Napoleon Bonaparte, which appears throughout the text, has been omitted from the index.